Your Spiritual Senses

Developing Sensitivity to God

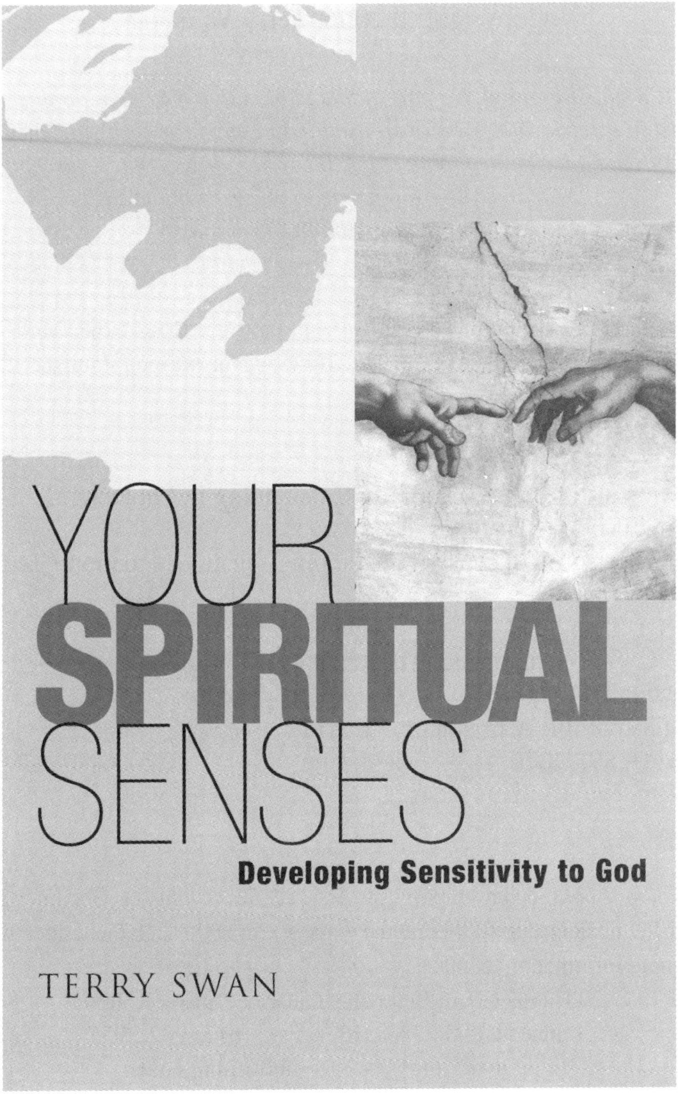

YOUR SPIRITUAL SENSES

Developing Sensitivity to God

TERRY SWAN

Guardian BOOKS

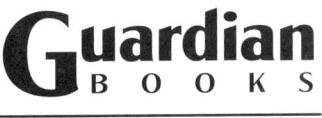

Belleville, Ontario, Canada

YOUR SPIRITUAL SENSES
Copyright © 2006, Terry W. Swan

All Rights Reserved. No part of this publication may be reproduced, stored in a retrieval system or transmitted in any form or by any means—electronic, mechanical, photocopy, recording or any other—except for brief quotations in printed reviews, without the prior permission of the author

All Scripture quotations are taken from the New King James Version. Copyright © 1979, 1980, 1982. Thomas Nelson Inc., Publishers.

Library and Archives Canada Cataloguing in Publication
Swan, Terry, 1953-
    Your spiritual senses : developing sensitivity to God / Terry Swan.
ISBN 1-55452-111-4
    1. Self-actualization (Psychology)--Religious aspects--Christianity.
    2. Spiritual life--Christianity. I. Title.
BV4319.S93 2006   248.4   C2006-906638-8

Guardian Books is an imprint of *Essence Publishing,* a Christian Book Publisher dedicated to furthering the work of Christ through the written word.. For more information, contact:
20 Hanna Court, Belleville, Ontario, Canada K8P 5J2
Phone: 1-800-238-6376 • Fax: (613) 962-3055
E-mail: info@essence-publishing.com
Web site: www.essence-publishing.com

Printed in Canada
by

I offer heartfelt thanks to God through Jesus Christ for "I once was blind, but now I see." Thanks to my wife for being the most spiritually sensitive individual I know personally. Thanks to my students, who consistently cause me to smile as I see them growing up towards God as flowers turn and reach towards the sunlight.

A special thanks is offered to Thomas Talbot for all his attentive, Christ-like dedication as he assisted in typing and compiling the book.

- Terry Swan

Table of Contents

1. Spiritual Sensitivity 9
2. Your Spiritual Senses 21
3. Sight—Spiritual Awareness 33
4. Hearing—Spiritual Discernment 45
5. Smell—Spiritual Cleansing 61
6. Taste—Spiritual Appetite 79
7. Touch Ministry 93
8. Wisdom—The Sixth Sense .103
9. Spiritual Frostbite 113
10. Spiritual Strength 121

By comparison with God's perfect understanding, we are like a man inside a barrel looking through a bunghole.

- R. R. Brown

We cannot too often think there is a never-sleeping eye which reads the heart and registers our thoughts.

- Francis Bacon

Jesus is God spelling himself out in language that man can understand.

- S. D. Gordon

John Baillie made it a practice to open his course on the "Doctrine of God" at Edinburgh University with these words:

Gentlemen, we must remember that in discussing God we cannot talk about him without his hearing every word we say. We may be able to talk about some of our fellows, as it were, behind their backs, but God is everywhere, yes, even here in this classroom. Therefore, in all of our discussions we must be aware of his infinite presence and talk about him, as it were, before his face.

Chapter One
Spiritual Sensitivity

God wants to communicate with you. And I would suspect that, by picking up and reading this book, you wish to communicate with God. How comforting it may be to discover that God has formed you in order to enjoy you and for you to have a vibrant interactive relationship. You are made to experience God, to be close to God, to know God. And a person with an experience always has an edge over a person with simply an idea or a philosophy.

Saint Thomas Aquinas was the most famous and brilliant of all the medieval theologians. He was able to dictate one book to a scribe, and while the man was writing down the sentence, Aquinas would turn to another scribe and dictate a sentence in a second book. Talk about the original multi-tasker!

His greatest work was known as the *Summa Theologiae*–the summary of theology. It was the comprehensive work of the study of God in his day or, perhaps, in any day. One day, during a service of Holy Communion, Thomas had a vision of God so powerful that he quit working altogether. His assistants urged him to complete the *Summa*, but he responded to their request by saying, "After what I have seen, all that I have written seems to me like so much straw."

Shortly after his glimpse of God, Thomas died. He no longer saw through a glass darkly but could look upon the light that enlightens every human being. The perfect communication and communion marred by the fall and consequent sin had no effect in heaven.

Immaculate Reception—Is Your Antenna Up?

When I train budding counselors in classes, I speak to them of becoming exquisite communicators. That is, counselors must develop a great sensitivity to what their clients say (and don't say), their voice inflection and body language. In the same vein, we too can develop a sensitivity to the presence of God. God is always revealing Himself to us. Consider these words from the psalmist:
The heavens declare the glory of God;
And the firmament shows His handiwork.
Day unto day utters speech,
And night unto night reveals knowledge.
There is no speech nor language
Where their voice is not heard.
Their line has gone out through all the earth,
And their words to the end of the world.[1]

A few years ago, there were billboards scattered throughout the United States with messages from God. Some guy had purchased the space and conducted an advertising campaign for God. Actually, the person responsible for these "messages from God" chose to remain anonymous. The Smith Agency in Ft. Lauderdale, Florida, launched the advertising campaign. Andrew Smith, the agency's president, said that an individual simply appeared in their office one day and hired them on the spot. He said that their agreement with this individual prohibited them from releasing his name, but he did say that the person is quite well known.

These fifteen messages signed "God" have appeared on billboards and buses:
1. Let's Meet at My House Sunday Before the Game.—God
2. C'mon Over and Bring the Kids.—God
3. What Part of "Thou Shalt Not..." Didn't You Understand?—God
4. We Need to Talk.—God
5. Keep Using My Name in Vain and I'll Make Rush Hour Longer.—God

6. Loved the Wedding, Invite Me to the Marriage.—God
7. That "Love Thy Neighbor" Thing, I Meant It.—God
8. I Love You… I Love You… I Love You.—God
9. Will the Road You're On Get You to My Place?—God
10. Follow Me.—God
11. My Way Is the Highway.—God
12. Need Directions?—God
13. You Think It's Hot Here?—God (During the summer)
14. Tell the Kids I Love Them.—God
15. Have You Read My #1 Best Seller? There Will Be a Test.—God[2]

It was a clever campaign and underscores a deep truth: God is always communicating messages to us.

A park ranger at Yellowstone National Park was leading a scouting group of hikers through the park. As the ranger was pointing out the various sites and flowers, he became irritated at the distracting noise made by his two-way radio, so he turned it off. As the group neared one of the fire towers, a lookout rushed up to them and asked why he hadn't responded to his messages. A grizzly bear had been spotted stalking the group of hikers, and he'd been trying to warn them.

Is *your* antenna up? There is an old gospel song entitled "Turn Your Radio On" in which we are implored to "tune in" and get in touch with God.

We not only have to make sure our antennas are up, we also have to be on the right wavelength. The channel is not hard to find if several elements are present, including a new birth, expectancy, humility, and a thirst for God.

A New Birth

John Wesley, founder of the Methodist movement, was punctilious to note that regeneration (a new birth) along with justification by faith were the two fundamental factors in the Christian faith.[3] He compares a new spiritual birth to a natural birth. Before a child comes into the world, she has eyes but cannot see.

She has ears but she can hear little. She has no knowledge of the outside world until birth when she sees light and objects and hears and experiences the world as all her senses function fully. To put it in Wesley's eighteenth century words:

> How exactly doth the parallel hold in all these instances? When a man is in a mere natural state, before he is born of God, he has, in a spiritual sense, eyes and sees not; a thick impenetrable veil lies upon them; he has ears but hears not; he is utterly deaf to what he is most of all concerned to hear. *His other spiritual senses are all locked up;* he is in the same condition as if he had them not. Hence he has no knowledge of God; no intercourse with Him; He is not at all acquainted with Him[4] (emphasis added).

Wesley goes on to contrast the new birth:

> But as soon as he is born of the spirit, there is a total change. Eyes and ears, heart and mind are opened. He sees the light of God's love with the face of Jesus Christ. He hears the inward voice of God saying, "Be of good cheer; thy sins are forgiven thee." He feels in his heart the mighty working of the Spirit of God. He grasps with his mind the truth of the Word and daily increases in knowledge. It is now that he is "properly said to live."[5]

Expectancy

When you are twice-born and part of the family, you will naturally expect that your Father will speak to you regularly. Thus, a desire must be present for this communication.

Don't fault yourself for not being good at this yet. John Paul Jackson has pointed out that no one is mature at birth. What is true in the natural realm is true in the spiritual realm. You're immature at the start and God doesn't despise your immaturity. You grow into maturity. In fact, God is as pleased with your first expectant attempts as a parent is with his or her toddler learning to take the first steps.

The first hymn I ever remember learning was taught to me by

my saintly Swedish paternal grandmother. At four years of age, I would join in singing what I called my hymn. I would sing,
> And he walks with me
> And he talks with me
> And he tells me I am his own
> And the joy we share
> As we tarry there
> None other has ever known.
>
> - In the Garden (C.A. Miles)

I called it my hymn because I mistakenly thought it referred to my name *Terry* when it mentioned the joy we share as we *tarry* there.

Never mind that it seemed misspelled to me. My first connection with a Christian hymn was about walking and talking with God. It made an indelible impression on me. To this day, of all the postures of prayer, I prefer to walk and talk with God. Spiritual sensitivity is about expecting that you can truly walk and talk, and God is walking and talking with you.

Years later as a young adult, the US Army, in its wisdom, sent me to be stationed in New York City. A small-town boy, from a rural area so far out in the country our zip code was E-I-E-I-O, gets moved to a city of eight million. I was a good soldier. I learned fast. I learned:

> If it moves you salute it.
> If it's on the ground, you pick it up.
> If you can't pick it up, paint it.

But the best part is what I learned through the churches in New York City. God was there to commune with even among the noise in the city that never sleeps. I grew in my knowledge of God through Norman Vincent Peale at Marble Collegiate Church in Manhattan. Near my base in Brooklyn, I attended a church pastored by Malcolm Smith, a most remarkable preacher.

Self-admittedly, Malcolm Smith did not have a great educational background. His primary formal education ended with elementary school. Each week he would pace before the Lord, walking and talking and imploring God to speak to him and through him. Each Sunday, God would answer that expectant faith-filled prayer and Reverend Smith would deliver deeply moving and insightful messages that drew us close to God.

Why should we be surprised when God answers these prayers? When you ask for God's presence, not just God's hand, you begin to see, and hear, and feel God all around you. And usually, if you do catch a glimpse of God, you don't stand for long. You fall on your face.

Occasionally in Scripture, God shows up to meet that expectation in dramatic fashion, as in Isaiah, the sixth chapter. Here we have Isaiah, a respected, righteous prophet, a consultant to three kings, who comes to the temple, because of the crisis of a king's death. He comes to seek God and he's not disappointed. God's awesome majesty and presence fill the temple and Isaiah, knowing he can't look upon God and live, falls to his face. While he can't see God, he hears the winged creatures flying around God's throne singing a hymn. These heavenly beings are singing a hymn composed in heaven by the very creatures who can see God.

Now I come from a tradition that loves to sing. In fact, we sing our theology. We ought to be able to appreciate all Christian music, new and old. Unfortunately, it's a point of contention in many churches. I have visited many churches where when I see the selection of hymns I think, "Wow! If the 1950s ever come back, this church will be ready for it!"

On the other end of the spectrum are churches that only sing contemporary praise songs. We were at a church in Nashville, Tennessee, where the young worship leader introduced the praise song as an "oldie." When the song came onto the projection screen, I looked at the copyright date and it was all of four years old! When I think oldie, I think of five centuries old like "A Mighty Fortress is Our God." That's an oldie.

Humans like to create music, and the music you listen to impacts how you think and feel. Having mentioned Nashville, two prominent sociologists found that people who listen to a lot of country-western music are prone to depression. Think of the themes: Tears in your beers. Can't trust happiness. My baby left me. If a country record contained backmasked lyrics, do you know what you happen if you played it backwards? You'd get your job back, your wife would come back, your dog would return…

But Isaiah doesn't hear a song written by earthly composers. It's a song from heaven by those who actually can look upon God. The winged creatures are singing, "Holy, Holy, Holy Lord God Almighty. The whole earth is full of your glory."

R. C. Sproul points out that this is an example of something quite rare in Scripture. When Jewish people wanted to emphasize something in Hebrew, they repeated it. If I am writing in English I might create emphasis by putting words in italics or capital letters or underscore the words. Hebrews, though, did it through repetition.

For example, when Jesus would get up to speak, He would begin by repeating the word *truly*. "Truly, truly I say unto you." He uses the word *Amain* from which we get our English word *Amen*. Amen usually appears at the end of a prayer. When you say *amen* you're saying "let this be true." Jesus uses amen at the beginning as if to say, "What I'm about to tell you is truly true."

While repetition occurs throughout Scripture, only one time is an attribute repeated thrice and it appears in Isaiah.[6] The winged creatures, the beings who can truly see God for who God is, sing that God is holy, holy, holy.

Isaiah just catches a glimpse of that holy presence before falling on his face. Surely he would never doubt ever again whether the holy God of the universe was interested in communicating with him.

Isaiah also becomes aware of his acute sinfulness, for he cries out, "Woe is me. I'm a man of unclean lips and I dwell among an unclean people." He sees that God is holy—and he is not. This leads to a third necessary element, which is humility, a right understanding of your relationship with God.

Humility; Meek is not Weak

One of my favorite Old Testament Scripture passages is Micah 6:8 where we're told:

> He has shown you, O man what is good;
> And what does the LORD requires of you.
> But to do justly,
> To love mercy,
> and to walk *humbly* with your God? (emphasis added)

In other words, we *already* know this. To walk with God, we must do so with humility. It's not rocket science, yet we resist humility. Perhaps being humble sounds like humiliation, and it does come from the same root. No one likes to be humiliated. Your family, who knows you well already, can keep you humble. A man and his wife went to church, and while kneeling at the altar, the man prayed out loud, "O Lord, make me successful and please keep me humble." His wife, kneeling beside him, chimed in with a corrective prayer, "O Lord, you make him successful, I'll keep him humble."

Genuine humility, though, is not something others do to us—it's something you and I do. In James we are told to "humble ourselves."[6] It's an imperative. It is within us. It is a work of grace that enables us to correctly see who we are in relation to an almighty God. The greatest in the kingdom of heaven have learned this lesson.[7]

In the Sermon on the Mount, Jesus declared, "Blessed are the poor in spirit."[8] To be poor in spirit means you recognize you are spiritually bankrupt without God. Jesus goes on to say, "Blessed are the meek."[9] To be meek is to note you can do nothing of lasting significance without God. Meek is not weak.

We tend to think we're in control of our own lives when in fact all it takes is one little germ, one wrong turn on the highway, one fall and that's it for our earthly existence. To believe we can manage our existence on our own is pride, which sets us against God. "God resists the proud but gives grace to the humble."[10] Pride is considered by theologians to be the core sin from which all other sins emanate. Pride is like bad breath. Everyone notices it except the one who has it. It is self-sufficiency. Pride changed angels into devils. Jonathan Edwards wrote that nothing sets a person so much out of the devil's reach as humility. Humility can turn men and women into angels. Thomas More wrote in poetic fashion that "Humility is that low, sweet root from which all heavenly virtues shoot."

Humility is Holy, Healthy, and Heaven-Sent

To be *holy* means to be set apart for God. It runs against the grain of the world to practice humility. It's currently popular vernacular to speak of individuals having "don't dis me" attitudes. Don't dis me means don't you dare disrespect me. You see plenty of that attitude as individuals boast, swagger, and draw attention to themselves.

Humility is the polar opposite. To follow Christ, to be in serious communion with God, means you will be disrespected. Our Lord was spit upon, mocked, jeered, humiliated, and made to hang upon a cross. The same may happen to us. So the admonition is to stay humble—or stumble. John Wesley was greatly impacted by William Law, who penned these words which I've framed in my office so I'll be constantly reminded:

> "Let every day, therefore, be a day of humility; condescend to all the weaknesses and infirmities of your fellow-creatures, cover their frailties, love their excellencies, encourage their virtues, relieve their wants, rejoice in their prosperity, compassionate their distress, receive their friendship, overlook their unkindness, forgive their malice, be a servant of servants, and condescend to do the lowest offices to the lowest of mankind."

Humility is good for the soul. Humility is healthy. Humble pie should be part of everyone's spiritual diet. The writer in Proverbs had it right:

> A man's pride will bring him low
> But the humble in spirit will retain honor.[11]

Just as too much sunshine makes a desert, so too much pride and success insulates us from the presence of God as well as from others. There's a Scottish saying that "pride and grace never reside in the same place."

It could be said that humility is heaven-sent. False humility is when we put ourselves down in a deprecating manner. This is not heaven-sent, Holy Spirit induced humility. "True humility," says Tyron Edwards, "is not an object, groveling, self-despising spirit; it is but a right estimate as God sees us."

It comes from God, and it enables us to walk and talk and enjoy the sweet presence of our Creator. When we cast down our spirits in true humility, it is, as John Mason suggests, like throwing a ball to the ground, which makes it rebound higher toward heaven. And when there are times we don't see or hear or feel God's presence, we don't panic, because we know God is not obligated to do so, nor are we entitled to it. It's a gift of grace. We come to understand that "when the heavens are as brass," it is God's prerogative to move us from being feeling-centered Christians to spiritually-centered, humble human beings who are content to wait on God.

Under the Influence

A final key element to initiating greater spiritual sensitivity is cultivating a God-intoxication. In Ephesians 5:15-21, the Apostle Paul speaks of being filled with the Spirit. An interesting contrast is made with the overindulgence of liquor. Isn't it interesting that these are called "spirits" as well?

Paul warns against the influence of spirituous liquors, which *dull our* senses. Conversely, being intoxicated with God heightens our sensitivity.

During my years in the active-duty military, I would occasionally be on evening barracks duty. Sometimes soldiers would come back from a night of partying and I would have to ascertain whether they were drunk or not. Of course, they'd always deny it, but I could tell by the way they walked, or talked, or sang, or didn't submit to authority as a good soldier should. So also, you can tell whether a person is under the influence of the Holy Spirit.

A person who is intoxicated staggers when he or she walks. A Christian overflowing with the Holy Spirit walks "circumspectly," according to Paul. It means you are sensitive and aware. You observe in a "circumference" around you what is going on.

Paul says a drunken person is a fool. A God-intoxicated person is wise. He or she knows the will of God.

An intoxicated person loses track of time. The apostle shows us that God-filled individuals "redeem the time."

Finally, Paul gets to the heart of the matter in the lives of people under the influence of the Holy Spirit. You can tell by a person's speech because one's words are always reflective of what's in the heart. Unsavory speech, gossip, rumors, and constant criticism all give a person's spiritual condition away.

During the Persian Gulf War, Iraqi troops would fire upon Americans from hidden sand dunes and other secret sites. What they didn't know at the time was that Americans had developed some untested, yet sophisticated equipment that could track down the source of the enemy's fire. Within thirty seconds, US troops tracked the coordinates and fired right back to where the shots had come from and killed the enemy. Word soon got around the Iraqi army. Shoot at the Americans and you'll get shot back at and killed.

I've wondered, what would happen if every time we shot at others by passing on a rumor, we got shot back? I bet it wouldn't be long before it would kill ungodly speech patterns.

Lastly, we are reminded that a Spirit-filled person is submissive. Generally, people under the influence of liquid spirits are selfish and obstinate—their worst selves. A fellow in New York State had been picked up several times for DUIs, driving under the influence, so the state took his license away. He got picked up yet again soon after for driving his lawn mower downtown while drunk! Here is an uncommitted person constantly trying to skirt the law rather than obey it.

Not so for individuals who want to walk with God. Their lives are characterized by submission to the known will of God.

So how are you doing? If you took a spiritual breathalyzer test, would we find you intoxicated with the Spirit of God? When you are filled with the Spirit, you are on your way to having your senses more spiritually attuned.

Lord, send me where Thou wilt, only go with me; lay on me what Thou wilt, only sustain me.

- Titus Coan

A mystic is anyone who believes that when you talk to God, God talks back.

- Frank Laubach

The human mind treats a new idea the way the body treats a strange protein; it rejects it.

- Biologist P. B. Medawar

Every man has a train of thought on which he rides when he is alone. The dignity and nobility of his life, as well as his happiness, depend upon the direction in which that train is going, the baggage it carries, and the scenery through which it travels.

- Joseph Fort Newton

You're unique…just like everyone else.

- From a bumper sticker

The intelligent man finds almost everything ridiculous, the sensible man hardly anything.

- Goethe

Chapter Two
Your Spiritual Senses

I was first introduced to the some of the rudiments of learning styles when, as a young professor, I took a test as part of preparation for teaching a college freshman seminar class. I sat in a classroom with a dozen other educators who were in training to specifically help first year at-risk college students. The test itself, even the name so long forgotten, covered learning styles as well as a number of other elements in communication. Upon completion of the exam, I was told to chart my scores on a graph that was provided.

Most people's scores show definite preferences and styles. Their charts display peaks and valleys and so look something like this:

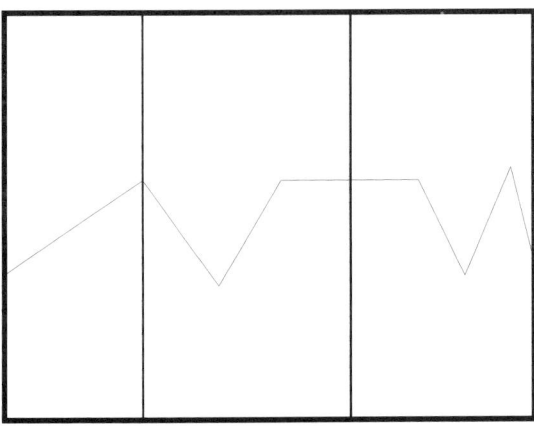

When I mapped out my totals on the graph. I was certain I

must have made a mistake somewhere. In fact, I turned to Dr. Matthews, a religion professor sitting next to me, and whispered that surely I had erred since my graph didn't seem like we had been told it would appear. I didn't understand the interpretation.

Dr. Matthews glanced over at my chart, which looked something like this:

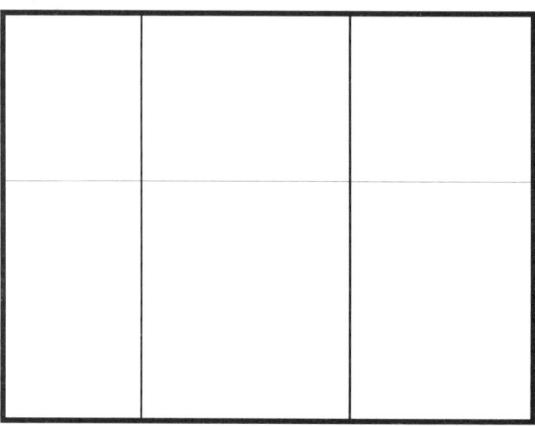

He quipped, "It appears you're brain-dead."

Of course I wasn't brain-dead. In fact, I was very much alive as I experienced what our psychologist friends call an "aha" moment concerning ourselves. I understood why I was an educator. I realized why college was the best ten years of my life. (I wasn't really a slow learner. I did graduate in four terms. It just happened to be the terms of Nixon, Ford, Carter, and Reagan!)

I am one of those unusual students who tend to learn in any setting. If the teacher uses a lot of visual representations, such as videos or the chalkboard, I learn. If the teacher never touches a piece of chalk or a video player but lectures well, tells stories, and follows a logical outline, I learn. If the teacher utilizes lots of interactive group learning or hands-on activities, I learn as well.

It naturally impacts my teaching styles. No wonder I gravitate towards a variety of methods. If I've had any effectiveness, it may well be that my diverse style contacts a greater number of students.

And you, dear reader, have your own specific perception

system. You have a unique learning style. It's the way God put you together.

All truth is God's truth and God's truth can only come to us through our senses. There are only five senses, and perhaps like me, while growing up, you were told by your parents on occasion, "You don't seem to have any sense at all sometimes!" I wanted to say, "I do too, Dad. I've got five of them." But I never said it, because smarting off was a major sin in our house and a lesson to the seat of the pants was a sensory experience I always wanted to avoid.

Learning styles enthusiasts have focused on the three major representational systems, of the five total, out of which usually one is primary. Your primary representational system says a great deal about how you process information. Information that comes our way usually comes in the forms of seeing (visual), hearing (auditory), or feeling (kinesthetic). With so much sensory information constantly coming our way, we learn over time to screen out the sensory overload that surrounds us. This style of selectively receiving and processing information is generally your preferred representational system.

Over half of us tend to be visuals. What you see is of greatest importance. You're more likely to be an avid reader, an internet-surfer, and a video renter. You use phrases such as "Can't you see what I'm saying?" and visual words like *focus, clear, picture, outlook,* and many others. You tend to be a list-maker and like to be surrounded by lots of images and colors in your office or study.

Auditories make up perhaps a quarter to a third of all of us. What you hear carries the greatest weight. Your own voice tends to rise and fall when you speak. You like to listen to music and teaching tapes. You utilize phrases such as "Can you just tune in?" and words like *listen, sound, rhythm,* and *amplify.* You don't like to be distracted as you focus on your studies or reading. You like to hear stories and prefer lectures with logical outlines. You enjoy group discussions.

Kinesthetics complete our groupings with roughly fifteen to twenty percent of all of us. Kinesthetics tend to learn by doing.

You have greater "body awareness" than most individuals. You prefer activities that involve movement and interaction. You use phrases like "Can you feel this?" and words like *touch, contact, sensitive,* and *stuck.* You're helped by routines and rituals in your day.

Mirror Christianity

As you can see, you are made to be a sensory being. You are a spirit who dwells in a human body while on this earth. Or, as Pierre Teilhard de Chardin, a French monk (1881–1955) wrote, "We are not just human beings having a temporal Spiritual experience. We are Spiritual beings having a temporal human experience."[1]

When you look in a mirror, you see your body, a sensory shell that contains your essence. Your body can be like insulation that drowns out spiritual sensitivity, or it can become a receptor. God is always trying to communicate with us, whoever we are and wherever we are. God's message, the good news, remains the same, but it is accommodated to the human condition so we can understand it. This does not mean God is subject to our limitations at all. It does mean that in your relationship with God, you will process that communication in a certain way.

My learning styles test showed me I learn and assimilate information in a variety of ways. Therefore, it makes sense that I enjoy experiencing God in a multitude of settings. I appreciate the beautiful visual setting of a liturgical sanctuary. I can enjoy a good sermon in a plain, quiet setting. I can participate in a worship service that has significant movement and emotion.

Beyond the visual, auditory, and kinesthetic senses, we furthermore recognize the two other senses that are important in our relationship with God. These are smell, or olfactory, and taste, or gustatory. All are significant in the Bible and can be used in connectivity to God. There are thousands of examples in Scripture, and below I listed just a single verse for each representational system and placed a spiritual moniker upon each sense.

Visual (Spiritual Awareness)

> Jesus answered and said to him, "Most assuredly I say to you, unless one is born again, he cannot see the kingdom of God."[2]

Auditory (Spiritual Discernment)

> He who has ears to hear, let him hear![3]

Kinesthetic (Spiritual Touch or Incarnational Ministry)

> And the Word became flesh and dwelt among us, and we beheld His glory, the glory as of the only begotten of the Father, full of grace and truth.[4]

Olfactory (Spiritual Cleansing)

> Therefore, having these promises, beloved, let us cleanse ourselves from all filthiness of the flesh and spirit, perfecting holiness in the fear of God.[5]

Gustatory (Spiritual Appetite)

> Oh, taste and see that the LORD is good;
> Blessed is the man who trusts in Him![6]

A part of spiritual maturity then would involve development of these senses so that you can better interpret God's message to you and through you. By utilizing the lens of spiritual senses, you can read Bible stories of mature saints such as Ezekiel in a new light. In Ezekiel's famous vision of the wheel at the start of his book in the Bible, the prophet, in the midst of spiritual hardness, ignorance, and cynicism, falls to his face and:

— *sees* a vision of a whirlwind and heavenly creatures;
— *hears* God's voice;
— *experiences* the hand of the Lord on him;
— *tastes* the scroll like honey.

A mature, obedient saint who walks with God for many years finds it easier to ascertain God's will and direction over time. Or, as the writer of Proverbs puts it, "But the path of the just is like the shining sun, that shines ever brighter unto the perfect day."7

God's lamp unto your feet and light unto your path becomes a more familiar friend over the years. You become more skilled at separating God's message from the stain of the world's messages that crowd and demand your attention in shrill fashion.

A beautiful prayer is attributed to Saint Patrick. It is called *Lorica*, named for a Roman coat of armor meant for the protection of the one wearing it.

> I arise today through God's strength to pilot me;
> God's might to uphold me,
> God's eye to look before me,
> God's word to speak for me,
> God's hand to guard me,
> Christ with me, Christ before me, Christ behind me,
> Christ in me, Christ beneath me, Christ above me,
> Christ on my right, Christ on my left,
> Christ when I lie down, Christ when I sit down,
> Christ when I arise,
> Christ in the mouth of everyone who speaks of me,
> Christ in every eye that sees me,
> Christ in every ear that hears me,
> I arise today
> through a mighty strength,
> the invocation of the Trinity.

Now, lets take a Spiritual Senses quiz to learn more about your own God-given primary representational system.

SPIRITUAL SENSES QUIZ

Check the statements listed that apply to you and total them as directed at the end. One point awarded for each checked statement.

___ 1. You often hear the still small voice of God speak to you in the quiet moments.

___ 2. Your body often reacts to the spiritual climate of a place.

___ 3. You prefer to pray with your eyes open.

___ 4. You enjoy listening to Christian teaching tapes and CDs.

___ 5. You prefer a plain sanctuary with little distraction from listening to the word of God and the sermon.

___ 6. You learn Christian lessons best by participating in activities.

___ 7. In worship settings, you tend to sway to the music.

___ 8. You're a people watcher in church.

___ 9. You tend to write down and journal your spiritual thoughts.

___ 10. You are quick to feel the presence of the Holy Spirit in a worship service.

___ 11. You prefer your minister to wear a plain suit on Sunday morning.

___ 12. When praying with others, you prefer to hold hands or touch them.

___ 13. You can run "movies" of events quite easily in your mind.

___ 14. When you meet someone new in church, you repeat his or her name aloud.

___ 15. You often tilt your head to one side or the other while listening to a sermon or Bible study.

___ 16. You can't sit for a long time without getting up and moving around.

___ 17. You've had visions of God or coming events.

___ 18. You enjoy liturgical services with lots of color, banners, and ornate design.

___ 19. You enjoy an interactive worship service where you can meet people and talk or pray with them.

___ 20. You prefer to pray with your eyes closed.

___ 21. You tend to tap your fingers to the beat of a hymn or praise chorus.

___ 22. You regularly hear an urgent prophetic word in your mind to exhort the church to get closer to God.

___ 23. You have detailed and spiritually significant dreams.

___ 24. The most important part of a worship service to you is the sermon.

___ 25. You help lead music on occasion, either singing or playing an instrument.

___ 26. You tend to learn best in Sunday School or Bible study when the teacher uses the chalkboard.

___ 27. You find it very meaningful to carefully observe the consecration of Holy Communion elements.

___ 28. You tend to hear yourself thinking on a sermon or scripture verses.

___ 29. You have a strong sense of awareness of evil.

___ 30. You look for the big picture when making decisions or moral choices.

___ 31. You listen carefully to announcements in church.

___ 32. You often hum praise songs or hymns in your head.

___ 33. It's important for you to feel physically comfortable in church (i.e. temperature, pews, etc.)

___ 34. You are quite intuitive.

___ 35. You like the church sanctuary or prayer room to be neat and clean.

___ 36. You are often moved by the words in special music at church.

___ 37. Music is what most draws you to a worship service.

___ 38. You prefer your minister to wear a robe and vestments during Sunday morning worship.

___ 39. You like to read Christian books.

___ 40. You base your first impression of people in church on what they say.

___ 41. You can often see things in your mind clearly.

___ 42. You'd rather tape or record messages rather than take notes.

___ 43. You prefer to serve in action-oriented ministries rather than contemplative, quiet prayer ministry.

___ 44. Your attention is more easily captured when the speaker uses props and visual arts.

___ 45. You find it easier to worship in a beautiful nature setting.

___ 46. You make "to-do" lists so you'll practice Christian obligations.

___ 47. You like to walk and pray outdoors.

___ 48. Sometimes you read aloud Bible passages.

___ 49. In worship, you like the words of hymns and scripture to be projected onto a screen.

___ 50. You like to raise your hands during worship.

___ 51. Sometimes God gives you a word to be shared with someone else.

1. A	27. V
2. K	28. A
3. V	29. K
4. A	30. V
5. A	31. A
6. K	32. A
7. K	33. K
8. V	34. K
9. V	35. V
10. K	36. A
11. A	37. K
12. K	38. V
13. V	39. V
14. A	40. A
15. A	41. V
16. K	42. A
17. V	43. K
18. V	44. V
19. K	45. V
20. A	46. V
21. K	47. K
22. K	48. A
23. V	49. A
24. A	50. K
25. K	51. A
26. V	

TOTAL YOUR SCORES

Visual   _____

Kinesthetic   _____

Auditory   _____

Highly visual persons tend to see visions and have significant, intricate dreams. They have a strong spiritual awareness—of others, of human need and of God's presence. Visuals enjoy worship services that have lots of visual stimulation such as banners, ornate design, statuary, and colors. They like to have the words to music on a screen where they can see them, and they actually take time to read the bulletin. They may well write down notes during the sermon and mark in their Bibles.

Auditory persons often hear God's voice in unexpected places. They look forward to the sermon and prefer more plain sanctuaries that won't hold distractions from listening to God's word. They may be more likely to pray with their eyes closed. They actually listen to the announcements and Scripture readings in church. Auditories have strong discerning gifts and have significant words to share with others.

Kinesthetics appreciate interactive worship services. Music draws them and they may be swaying to the music or lifting up hands. They often feel great empathy for others in need and have a keen sense of good and evil or right and wrong. Kinesthetics sometimes sense a spiritual climate within their own bodies.

While we list these attributes in generalities, most individuals have some level of all representational systems in their make-up. Do make special note, though, of your primary system.

The greatest thing a human soul ever does in this world is to see something and tell what he saw in a plain way. Hundreds of people can talk for one who can think, but thousands can think for one who can see. To see clearly is poetry, prophecy, and religion—all in one.

- John Ruskin

I have talked with people whose eyes are full of light but who see nothing in the wood, sea, or sky, nothing in city streets, nothing in books. Their souls voyage through this enchanted world with a barren stare.

- Helen Keller

The Christian on his knees sees more than the philosopher on tiptoe.

- Dwight L. Moody

In darkness there is no choice. It is light that enables us to see the difference between things, and it is Christ who gives us light.

- C. T. Whitmell

I now send you to open their eyes, in order to turn from darkness to light, and from the power of Satan to God.

- Acts 26:17-18

Chapter Three
Sight
Spiritual Awareness

Your eyes. How precious they are. When people are asked to vote which body part they would least want to lose, invariably the "eyes" have it. In the Bible, eyes are enormously important as well, for in a spiritual sense, they refer to spiritual awareness.

In John the third chapter there is the famous story of Nicodemus, the respected teacher who came by night to visit Jesus. This was, of course, the original Nick at Night. Nicodemus is told by Jesus that unless he was born again he could not see the kingdom of God. In other words, unless a person has a salvation experience, he or she can never fully understand what Christianity is all about.

It can't be examined on its own and make any sense without spiritual awareness. How can it be that this man Jesus who lived briefly, died violently, and rose unexpectedly has anything to do with one's life? It just won't register without the prevenient grace of God. Before salvation, God gives a person just enough light to understand that he or she needs God. The darkness in one's life blurs the faded image of God within.

Jesus called the eye "the lamp of the body." He said,

> The lamp of the body is the eye. If therefore your eye is good, your whole body will be full of light. But if your eye is bad, your whole body will be full of darkness. If therefore the light that is in you is darkness, how great is that darkness![1]

If one's eye is dark, it distorts the whole picture. You get an inaccurate portrait of reality.

Sir Percival Lowell was likely the planet's most eminent astronomer as the world entered the twentieth century. Based on earlier work in the late 1800s by some European astronomers, Lowell became convinced there were straight lines across the surface of Mars. He believed the straight lines were canals that showed proof of intelligent beings on Mars.

Captivated by this theory, Lowell devoted much of the rest of his life squinting into his giant telescope in his Arizona conservatory and drawing maps of the canals. We know today, of course, there are no such canals nor even straight lines.

The explanation? Sir Percival Lowell had a rare eye disease where he could see the blood vessels in his own eye. What he thought were canals were just the veins in his own blood vessels! This disease today is often referred to as "Lowell's syndrome."

Before Christ, the light of the world, enters our lives, we are all struck with the malady of "Lowell's syndrome." Renowned psychologist Albert Ellis says the world is our mirror. We see the world in a manner we wish to and collect evidence to support that sense of reality. Before Christ is Lord, we are our own gods. Therefore, we see the world in an egocentric, selfish manner.

Furthermore, our sense of darkness is supernaturally shaded by an evil one who is referred to by Paul as "the god of this age." Paul elaborates:

> But even if our gospel is veiled, it is veiled to those who are perishing, whose minds the god of this age has blinded, who do not believe, lest the light of the gospel of the glory of Christ, who is the image of God, should shine on them.[2]

When you live in darkness, then your attention can be captivated by even the most faint of lights. In Georgia, a man sued the electric company. He was going along on a motorcycle, sitting back in his seat going past many electric light poles next to the road. In his claim in court the man stated, "I was mesmerized by all the light poles. The road turned left but the poles kept going straight and I just went on with them and crashed into the pine trees…"

So he sued them! Isn't that just indicative of people? They keep going the direction they choose to and then blame the consequences on others!

God gives only enough light to the person who is outside Christ so that he or she can see to turn the right direction. But it still comes down to a conscious choice of what lies before you. The same sun that melts butter hardens clay. The same gospel that causes one's heart to melt and eyes to weep may only harden another's resolve to not give in to God.

In one of the clearest verses in the New Testament, the Apostle Paul tells the Corinthian church in his first letter how little the person outside of God understands the nature of spiritual things. Paul wrote:

> But the natural man does not receive the things of the Spirit of God, for they are foolishness to him; nor can he know them, because they are spiritually discerned.[3]

Each day you pass by, work with, talk to, and perhaps live with people who are as if they are in a spiritual fog. Jesus rather distinctly divided up the world into two groups. There are those who believe and those who don't. It all hinges on seeing the kingdom. What are you seeing?

A Matter of Perspective

People are likely to rationalize away their behaviors no matter how poorly they're performing. It's a matter of perspective. They're not unlike the young pitcher who thought he was hot stuff when called from the minors to pitch for the New York Mets in 1960. However, in his initial start, he walked the first seven batters so Coach Casey Stengel removed him from the game. The rookie stormed to the dugout mumbling, "How do you like that dumb coach Stengel? He takes me out of the game just when I have a no-hitter going!"

Let's create a scenario. What happens to the individual pitching a no-hitter in life? Perhaps there are some outward financial successes, but the person has no peace and is failing at relationships and the things that matter most in life. In the midst of their darkness, there is a tug on the heart. They see a glimmer of light. If the eye is spiritual awareness, of what do they become aware?

We can ascertain this answer from another well known gospel story.[4] Early in Jesus' ministry he was teaching near the lake of Gennesarat. So many people crowded around him that Jesus got into Simon Peter's boat to teach the multitude. When he was done speaking he told Peter to let the fishing nets out again. Although Peter initially protests, he does what Jesus recommends (which is always a good thing to do!)

You know the story. Even though they had fished all night without success, now every fish in the sea of Galilee seems to jump into their nets. In fact, the ships were weighted down so much they began to sink.

What is most fascinating is Peter's response. You'd think it might be gratitude or perhaps an invitation to set up a joint Jesus-and-Peter fishing company. Instead, Peter falls on his knees and asks Jesus to leave because he is such a sinful man.

Simon Peter's initial spiritual awareness is that Christ is holy and he himself isn't. This is true for all of us. Even as the light dawns on us that God loves us, we also become acutely aware of sin, the dark places in our lives.

There's a French proverb that says, "In the dark, all cats are gray." When in darkness, standards are indistinguishable. It's easy to look around and compare yourself to others and rationalize that you're not so bad. But then there are those moments of real clarity where you see things as they are.

I have a former college student who is a very fine Christian woman. She said coming out of high school in the 1960s she really didn't believe there was that much evil. Though she'd been raised in a Christian home, she got away from God. As a child of the sixties, she began to believe that people were all really good down deep. If you could just join hands with people of all backgrounds on a hillside and sing the Coke song, the Age of Aquarius would be ushered in, the world would live in perfect harmony, and everything would be fine.

One summer away from college, she spent the whole three months bumming around Europe. One night, she was in downtown Amsterdam where she had a real Kodak moment.

Everywhere she looked, she commented, it seemed a scene from hell:
- Drug-addicted people stumbling around;
- Drunken persons passed out;
- Legalized prostitutes calling out from the windows;
- Thefts and assaults committed right in front of her eyes.

Evil. That's all she could see that night in a society that had distanced itself from God. That experience drove her back to God in Christ Jesus.

When ABC's Ted Koppel spoke at the Duke University commencement, he offered some enlightened words on the subject. He said:

We've actually convinced ourselves that slogans will save us. Shoot up if you must but use a clean needle. Enjoy sex whenever and with whomever you wish but wear a condom.

No! The answer is no! Not because it isn't cool or smart or because you might end up in jail or dying in an AIDS ward but no because its wrong. In its purest form, truth is not a polite tap on the shoulder. It is a howling reproach. What Moses brought down from Mount Sinai were not the ten suggestions.

Koppel is asserting that in those moments of clarity, you see truth and it isn't always pleasant. This is why in Christianity you hear so much about the blood of Christ that forgives all sin and deception.

When you're blind, you only need one antidote and that is the power to see. And what you see first of all is a loving and holy God and that you're separated by a chasm called sin. Upon repentance and the placement of faith in Christ for forgiveness and salvation, you begin to see life with new spiritual eyes. Your spiritual awareness is beginning to change.

Step Into The Light

Arthur Rubenstein, the famous conductor, was once so depressed he decided to end his life. He always appeared so composed in public, but his private life was in shambles. He had a smile on the outside, yet no smile on the inside. He went to his closet looking for a rope and the closest thing to a rope was his bathrobe belt. Then, in his exact words, Arthur Rubenstein said:

> I took that bathrobe belt, made a slip knot in it, put it around my neck, climbed on a chair, tied the belt around the beam in the garage, and I jumped...The knot let go and I fell to my knees. When I finally got up, I walked out of the garage, pulled the knot loose, and threw it off and stepped outdoors. Suddenly I was surrounded by the beauty of life everywhere. It was beautiful. Sunshine, nature, the sky. And I've loved life ever since.

This is the second element of which you become aware. God's presence surrounds you. You've been cleansed and now you have a new sensitivity to God. Jesus put it this way in the Beatitudes: "Blessed are the pure in heart, for they shall *see* God."[5]

You discover a beauty present in God's world around you. God was always there, you just didn't notice it. For example, look at this statement:

GODISNOWHERE

You could interpret it as God is nowhere or God is now here. It depends on what you see.

If you ever purchased a new car, you suddenly become aware of all the other same models out on the road while you're driving. If you looked around to find five items with the color red, you'll find the color jumping out at you in books, pillows, paintings, or nature etc. You were developing a "red" mindset.

Before crossing the line of faith and stepping into the light, God seemed strongly absent from all the details. We simply lacked a "God" mindset. When we develop this sensitivity, we become aware of God everywhere. Jesus commented on this to his disciples when he said, "A little while longer and the world will see Me no more, but you will see Me. Because I live, you will live also."[6]

You see God and God sees you. The old hymn says "His eye is on the sparrow and I know he watches me." Peter Marshall noted that

> If God is not in your typewriter as well as your hymnbook, there is something wrong with your religion. If God does not enter into your kitchen, there is something wrong with your kitchen. If you can't take God into your recreation, there is something wrong with your play. We believe in a God of the heroic. What we need most is a God of the humdrum, the commonplace, the everyday.

A Radiant Life

Next, we note in spiritual awareness we begin to see that others observe us. People notice something different about you as you walk as light in the darkness. In fact, many decisions will be made about God based on you. For you're writing a fifth gospel. Most individuals will never read Matthew, Mark, Luke, and John, so the gospel they'll read is the one displayed by your life. And you'll never know when people are watching you.

When my children were small, we participated in a missions conference at a grand old downtown hotel in a large city. My obligations were done in the morning, so I took my two kids swimming at the big deep pool on the second story of the hotel. Meanwhile, my wife, Cinda, went down to the first lower level of the hotel to make dinner reservations at the restaurant.

As she stood in line at the restaurant desk to make the reservations, she saw two large picture windows that showed right underwater in the large pool, much like a human aquarium. Suddenly, there appeared her husband going by the window, blissfully swimming along, unaware that all those people were watching him. Just then my daughter came along underwater and playfully tugged down my swim trunks (fortunately not too far down!)

You would think the one place you'd be safe from public scrutiny would be deep underwater. But there were people watching my every move, including my wife. Jesus did say that we are like a city on a hill that can't be hidden.[7] Your very countenance will give you away.

My paternal grandfather suffered from and eventually died from the complications of Parkinson's disease. One of its symptoms is called a "facial mask" in which the face takes on a stiff, plastic appearance with a flat effect, lacking much expression. Underneath, though, was a heart of gold, filled with goodness and kindness that shone through. You could see the light and love of God in his eyes.

Charles William Elliot, former president of Harvard University, had a birthmark on his face that bothered him greatly. As a young man, he was told that surgeons could do nothing to remove it. Someone described that moment as "the dark hour of his soul."

Elliot's mother gave him this helpful advice: "My son, it is not possible for you to get rid of that hardship…But it is possible for you, with God's help, to grow a mind and soul so big that people forget to look at your face."

Our countenance along with corresponding conduct will convince people that our religion is real. People will see you as you've become, not who you were.

Needing a Second Touch

Finally, in our new spiritual awareness we start to see people as Christ does. Human needs surround you.

Wherever Jesus went while on the earth, he healed many people from blindness. He healed individuals in different ways, such as touching, use of spittle and mud, or simply speaking healing.

In one case he had to touch a blind man twice so he could see.[8] When Jesus first touched him, the man claimed he could see men as trees walking. In other words, the images of people were fuzzy and distorted. Jesus then touched him a second time and then he saw clearly.

Before conversion we tend to see people like trees walking. We don't really notice people and their needs and pain, and we don't want to see it. They just walk by like faceless people.

When you begin to see as Christ, you see clearly how much they need him. If you continue to do this, you can develop a sensitivity where at times God may give you insights into people's lives even as you look at them. As we mature, we begin to walk as the Apostle Paul suggested. We walk circumspectly, wisely, and carefully observing all of life.[9] You see God working, and that fills you with faith. You become, in Robert Schuller's words, a possibility thinker.

Yes, eyesight is precious. To be able to see is a blessing. To have your sight re-born so that you have spiritual awareness is a far greater blessing.

When Nathaniel was astonished that Jesus had seen him under the tree, Jesus promised a greater blessing of sight. Jesus said,

> "Most assuredly, I say to you, hereafter you shall see heaven open, and the angels of God ascending and descending upon the Son of Man."[10]

This promise of spiritual awareness is ours as well.
Three special thoughts for highly visible people:

1) Guard your eyes. Since the eye is indeed the lamp of the body, "watch what you watch" on television and the internet and in movies. Job determined he would be careful about what he looked at and even made a vow before God: "I have made a covenant with my eyes; Why then should I look upon a young woman?"[11]

It's always better to shield your eyes before viewing negative visually stimulating images than to deal with the repercussions of gazing too long at something unseemingly later.

2) Fill your eyes and mind with good things. Posters, an open Bible, scriptures taped to your desk, mirror, or car dash always lead you to higher ground.

3) Pay attention to how God may speak to you through your visual receptors in unusual ways. This may come through billboards, newspaper headlines, a commercial, or when people-watching. Pay attention, even when asleep, to what images regularly appear in your dreams.

A holy life is a voice; it speaks when the tongue is silent and is either a constant attraction or a perpetual reproof.

-Robert Leighton

The hearing ear and the seeing eye, the LORD has made them both.

- Proverbs 20:12

Take away everything I have, but do not take away the sweetness of walking and talking with the King of Glory!

- John Stam—a martyr

How rare to find a soul still enough to hear God speak.

- Fenelon

No heart thrives without much secret converse with God, and nothing will make amends for the want of it.

- John Berridge

Solid food belongs to those who are of full age, that is, those who by reason of use have their senses exercised to discern both good and evil.

- Hebrews 5:14

Chapter Four
Hearing Spiritual Discernment

Hearing has to do with spiritual discernment. Many times in the Gospels, Jesus said, "He who has ears, let him hear." We all have the ability to hear. Jesus was talking about a discerning ability to hear God's voice among other voices. It takes time and prayer and obedience to gain this level of maturation. To use the words of the Hebrews passage that began this chapter, one must "exercise his or her senses."

Little Samuel in the Bible heard a voice call his name three times in the night, and each time he ran to Eli the priest, thinking he was speaking to him. The third time Samuel came to inquire why the priest had spoken out to him, Eli discerned something his small protégé had not yet come to fully recognize. God was talking to Samuel. Eli told Samuel to lie and wait and when he heard God's voice he was to say, "Speak, for your servant hears." God indeed did give a word to Samuel, and it was about the destruction of Eli's household![1]

At age seven, like Samuel, I heard God's still small voice in the middle of the night. According to my mother's diary, I went into her room and told her that when I grew up I was to become a minister. Unlike Samuel, I wasn't wearing a linen ephod. I made my announcement wearing my Batman pajamas.

It was a most significant moment in my spiritual maturation, for from then on I knew there was a calling and destiny on my life. I would attend my little Lutheran church and sit in the very front row in front of the pulpit so I could observe and hear everything our fine pastor said and did. And then, since Lutherans (as in most denominations) sit in the back pews, I would be the first to be directed out of the church by the ushers walking past several empty pews directly behind me. I would later discover this is a corollary benefit when you want to get to the buffet line early for Sunday brunch!

There's a reason God gave you two ears and one mouth. We should be very good at hearing. However it takes years to begin to develop this spiritual sense. Most of us have been raised on thirty-second commercials and twenty-two-minute sitcoms and therefore have short attention spans. Eventually, though, we start to recognize the voice of God among the other clamoring voices that surround us.

Do You Hear What I Hear?

In an interview with King Charles, Joan of Arc spoke of the strange voices she heard. Charles, irritated, said that the voices should come to him, the king, and not to a mere subject. Joan answered, "They do come to you; but you do not hear them. If you prayed from your heart and listened, you would hear the voices as well as I do."

There are at least three levels of spiritual discernment where we must learn to separate God's voice from the others. First, it is a *voice of salvation*.

Have you ever noticed how we are usually surrounded by noise? Television, radios, cars, machines, airplanes, and conversations are all around us. A consistent barrage of noise can stain us and distract us.

We have the ability to listen at about 800 words per minute. We can talk at about 125 to 175 words per minute. If you're a fast-talking Yankee, you might be able to spew out words at 250 words per minute. Obviously, we can hear a great deal more than we're totally cognizant of at any point. I still continue to be amazed at college students who study with earphones on blasting out their favorite brand of music. I wonder how much they actually retain.

Think of how much you retain from hearing a sermon or a lecture. Perhaps you recall a story or a joke or a visual representation that added to your sensory memory. At one of the universities I attended, an experiment was conducted by the psychology department to ascertain how well students were listening in large lecture classes. With the professors' permission, psychology students burst into fifty large lecture classes, stopped the class activities and asked the students to write down on a piece of paper what they were thinking about the moment before the class was stopped.

As it turned out, only twelve percent of the college students were actually listening to their professors. The greatest number of students were fantasizing, a form of disassociation from their environment. They were listening to stories made up in their own minds! This ability to listen to more than one thing at once can actually keep us from the most precious thing in the world—our salvation. If our hearing is too distracted, we miss the world's most important message.

We are saved by faith. We are told by the Apostle Paul, "Faith comes by hearing, and hearing by the word of God."[2]

Right now we live in a culture that is shouting down the Christian message in a thousand different ways. While not wanting to return to any earlier time, it is obvious that not long ago, movies drew us to heroes and displayed dignity of the human spirit. Music often had lyrics that called you to loftier thoughts.

Today, this is rare. People typically don't flock in movie lines to see uplifting tales nor do they increase CD sales of classical music. Discerning the voice of salvation paves the way for all other levels of hearing God. It is the door, the entry point. Jesus, as recorded in John's Gospel, once said, "He who is of God hears God's words; therefore you do not hear, because you are not of God."[3]

Jesus also said,

"But he who enters by the door is the shepherd of the sheep. To him the doorkeeper opens, and the sheep hear his voice; and he calls his own sheep by name and leads them out. And when he brings out his own sheep, he goes before them; and the sheep follow him, for they know his voice. Yet they will by no means follow a stranger, but will flee from him, for they do not know the voice of strangers."[4]

When you're familiar with the voice of the Shepherd who leads your life, you are able to pause and discern his words from other voices demanding your attention. Recognizing the voice of salvation is to resist the clarion call of universalism that says all roads lead to God. It sidesteps relativism that suggests all morals are simply a construct of culture. It rejects humanism that puts human beings at the center of the world, not God. A discerning ability is necessary to hear the words that lead to faith.

In the midst of a confused, clamoring culture, the voice of salvation has not changed. It remains the gospel, the good news and the ultimate answer to the world's problems.

The Voice of True Religion

A second level of discernment might be called the *voice of true religion*. We so often have difficulty hearing this voice. Jesus, in his parable on the Sower and the Seed, described three unfruitful responses people have to God's word, which is God's voice:

1) Some don't understand what they've heard, and so Satan steals it out of their hearts.
2) Others are excited and joyful about becoming Christ-followers, but when persecuted, they cave in.
3) For yet others, the cares of this world (voices of this world) and deceitfulness of riches choke what they've heard, and they become unfruitful.[5]

Note that for the last group, it didn't say they lost their salvation. They just became unfruitful. They didn't mature as believers. They heard the word and then over time lost the discerning ability to live as Christ commanded his followers.

Paul told Timothy a time would come when believers would have "itchy" ears. This word literally means tickling; in this case, a distraction from the truth.[6]

Social scientist and pollster George Barna has pointed out that twenty-first-century American Christians increasingly look like their non-churchgoing neighbors. On any number of ethical and social practices there is no significant difference. It is entirely possible for people to come to church Sunday after Sunday and listen to the most remarkable stories in humankind and have them fall upon deaf ears. Their ears might as well be stuffed with cotton, for what is heard does not appear to make a significant translation into practice.

Douglas Meeks has pointed out that when Jewish families practice the Seder meal at Passover, the children are to ask as part of the ritual, "Why do we live this way?" He notes that today's children rarely ask that question of their parents. The reason: the parents often don't live very differently from the culture.

This doesn't mean the practice of church attendance by itself isn't important. There was an elderly, nearly deaf man who came for church services faithfully each week. When someone asked why he came to church when he couldn't hear, his reply was classic. He said, "I just want my neighbors to know whose side I'm on."

Perhaps he couldn't hear well physically, but he could hear well spiritually. The voice of true religion can only be heard by one whose ears are tuned into station W-SON. If you listen long enough to other voices, static enters in and you find yourself focused on W-SIN.

A well-known writer, speaker, and world leader once said, "If you repeat lies long enough, people come to believe them as the truth." This man consistently expressed that his country was superior and should rise to dominate the world and that other groups such as Jews were inferior. Fifty-million casualties and one terrible global war later, everyone could see the impact of who and what you are listening to in your mind. Of course, I'm referring to Adolf Hitler.

To whom are you listening? Who is on target? Three opinions from experts in years past underscore the significance of this question.

The first opinion comes from Charles Duell, head of the US

Patent office in 1899. He opined, "Everything that can be invented, has been invented."

A second opinion comes from Rober Milliken, 1923 Nobel Peace Prize winner in Physics, who said, "There's no likelihood that man will ever tap the power of the atom."

A third and final projection is from Henry Warner, who was President of Warner Brothers Motion Picture Studio in 1927, when talking movies were just coming out. He said, "Who wants to hear actors talk?"

What did these three men have in common? They were all dead wrong.

Are you listening to God's word or that of experts? We can appreciate and learn from skillful, thoughtful individuals, but would you listen to a celebrity on a talk show discuss her advice for relationships when she has had four divorces?

Do you listen when former athletes tell you to drink their brand of beer in one commercial while the next commercial has another famous athlete telling you to stay off drugs. Talk about cognitive dissonance!

David Wilkerson, the well-known Pentecostal preacher, was at one time a twenty-seven-year-old pastor of a small church in Pennsylvania. Every night he would sit in front of the television watching late night-talk shows. One evening after another boring time of TV viewing, a revolutionary thought came to him. What in the world am I listening to? What if instead of listening to TV talk-show hosts I listened to the God of the universe in prayer?

He decided, as a "fleece before the Lord," to place his television set for sale in the want ads and asked God to have a buyer purchase it within an hour of the paper coming out on the streets. Sure enough, within the hour, a buyer called to inquire about his TV. David hadn't even had time to think of a selling price. When he named it, the caller on the other end said he'd buy it, without even seeing the TV.

From then on, David Wilkerson's ministry influence skyrocketed. He would from then on use his time to listen to the true voice and the world was changed for the better.

It was Job who said, "Does not the ear test words?"[7] We need spiritual discernment to know how to live as Christians in the twenty-first century.

When King Josiah had the temple repaired, the workers found the book of the law. When God's word was read in his presence, he discerned the true voice of religion, repented, and acted upon it with all the Jewish people.[8] This leads us to a third level of discernment, which is the *voice of obedience*.

The Voice Of Obedience

God's voice calls us to salvation, to be part of the forever family. God's voice gives us clear words about how to live as a son or daughter of God. Responding to God's special instructions to you is the voice of obedience.

Francis Schaeffer was one of the great Christian leaders of the twentieth century. As a young man, he and his little family needed housing for a transition year in their lives, but they had little money in the bank. While Francis was praying about the matter, he heard an audible voice that didn't seem to come from inside his head. The voice simply said, "Uncle Harrison's house."

This didn't make sense to Francis Schaeffer, even though it was clearly what he'd heard. He had little contact with his Uncle Harrison and had never received anything from him. Yet the voice was so direct and clear he decided to obey and write his uncle, asking what he planned to do with his house over the next year. His uncle wrote back to say he planned to live with his brother for the next year and offered Francis and his family occupancy of the house rent-free.

There's a story of a captain of a ship who looked into the dark night and saw faint lights in the distance. Immediately he told his signalman to send a message: "Alter your course 10 degrees south."

Promptly a return message was received: "Alter *your* course 10 degrees north."

The captain was angered; his command had been ignored. So

he sent a second message: "Alter your course 10 degrees south—I am the captain!"

Soon another message was received: "Alter your course 10 degrees north—I am Seaman Third Class Jones."

Immediately the captain sent a third message, knowing the fear it would evoke: "Alter your course 10 degrees south—I am a battleship."

Then the reply came: "Alter your course 10 degrees north—I am a lighthouse."

Obedience by faith signals a maturity in believers. Recognizing and responding to the voice keeps us from crashing.

Moses wrote: "The word is very near you, in your mouth and in your heart, that *you may do it*.[9]

In fact, Jesus compared people who were not obedient to God's direction like a foolish man who built his house on sand and the winds and rain knocked it down.[10] We must learn to be obedient to the still small voice.

Isaiah wrote,

> Your ears shall hear a word behind you, saying, "This is the way, walk in it. "Whenever you turn to the right hand or whenever you turn to the left."[11]

This is beyond obedience to God's word. It is a reference to obedience in the very special claims God places on your life. Or as one speaker put it, it was his "short leash" in service to God.

In the quiet moments, in times of prayer and deep responding to deep, what does God specifically say to you? What do you hear regarding

- your thought life,
- your use of time,
- you priorities,
- your spending, or
- the words you speak?

Listen, for God indeed speaks. And if we love God, we obey God.

Static On Your Line

When I was a small child, my teacher would arrange the class to sit in a circle and we'd play a game called "Telephone." The teacher whispered a simple sentence of a few words into ear of the child nearest to her and gave directions for each child to pass on the message he or she heard. You can imagine the results! By the time the message made it around the class, it was so distorted that, perhaps at best, one or two words from the original sentence were included.

Obviously, static gets in our line. As we listen to messages, our own filter distorts what is being said to us. What can get in the way of our hearing God?

Distraction is one reason. Bishop A. Quayle, the story goes, went to bed one night, but sleep escaped him because of his distractions over problems he could not solve. Then he heard the voice of God speak: "Quayle, you go to bed. I'll sit up the rest of the night."

Emotions are yet another obstacle. Just because we *feel* strongly about something doesn't mean it's God.

At the transfiguration of Jesus, Peter became excited at seeing Moses and Elijah present with Jesus. Who wouldn't? But when Peter spoke out of the flesh with an idea to build three tabernacles, even God had to speak—a voice came out of a cloud saying, "This is My beloved Son. *Hear Him!*" (emphasis added)[12]

Unwillingness also hampers our ability to hear God. Jesus would often start his messages by inviting those who had an ear to hear. Lack of receptivity is like putting your antenna down. You don't hear, because you really don't want to hear God. Are your plans and timetable taking precedence over God's? Too often, we run ahead with our own blueprints for life and then ask God to sprinkle holy water on our human-made projects!

Human logic can be an impediment as well. God doesn't always work in a manner consistent with our reason. God-sense isn't necessarily logical to the human mind.

"For My thoughts are not your thoughts, Nor are your ways My ways," says the LORD. "For as the heavens are higher than the earth, So are My ways higher than your ways, And My thoughts than your thoughts."[13]

It is presumptuous of us to assume that the God of the universe must conform to our plans or our way of thinking. On occasion, our own rationale may become the very hurdle we have to overcome.

Rebellion is the most significant obstruction of them all. It is the decision to go our own way even when we know it's sinful. When we are guilty of this, not only do we not hear God but God chooses not to hear us.

> Behold, the LORD's hand is not shortened,
> That it cannot save;
> Nor His ear heavy
> That it cannot hear.
> But your iniquities have separated you from your God;
> And your sins have hidden His face from you,
> So that He will not hear.[14]

Sin is the primary static that distorts our messages from God. When we quiet ourselves before God and we become aware of a sin we have committed, we need to confess it and ask forgiveness. The line is re-opened, or as Isaiah put it:

> He awakens My ear
> To hear as the learned
> The Lord GOD has opened My ear;
> And I was not rebellious,
> Nor did I turn away.[15]

God desires to speak to us and does so through a clean conduit, a consecrated vessel.

Hearing Aids

> Prayer at its highest is a two-way conversation and for me the most important part is listening—to God's replies.
>
> - Frank Laubach

There are a number of "hearing aids" that can assist us to better discern God's voice.

We listen *expectantly*. We are not laying hold of God's reluctance, but rather God's willingness to engage in conversation with us. We can expect to receive illumination. God will make things clear to us.

"Call to Me and I will answer you, and show you great and mighty things, which you do not know."[16]

The key is expectation. Do you wait for God's answers?

When a little girl had finished her evening prayers, she remained at her beside for some time. Finally her mother told her to get into bed. "I was just waiting," the girl protested, "to see if God had anything to say to me."

We listen *scripturally*. The word of God is one of the Bible's appropriate titles. James Alexander has commented that "the study of God's word, for the purpose of discovering God's will, is the secret discipline which has formed the greatest character."

Hearing God Scripturally is not unlike learning a new language, which Rabbi Daniel Lapkin refers to as "the Lord's Language." We not only learn the words, but the words in context. Just as you'd spend many hours learning a new language, so you come to know the language of the Bible. Then, when you hear God's voice speaking through the words, you understand the context.

While Augustine was still living a life of sin and debauchery, he was nonetheless actively engaged in discussing Christianity, though not yet committed to Christ. One day he was sitting under a tree in a garden, feeling the anguish of his internal struggle, when he heard a child's voice singing, "Take up and read. Take up and read."

Augustine picked up the nearest book, a copy of the Bible, and casually flipped open the pages. His eyes fell upon Romans 13:13-14, which reads,

> Let us walk properly, as in the day, not in revelry and drunkenness, not in lewdness and lust, not in strife and envy. But put on the Lord Jesus Christ, and make no provision for the flesh, to fulfill its lusts.

To Augustine, it was the direct voice of God. After nearly ten years of exploring Christianity, he encountered Christ speaking to him about his way of life. Augustine was truly converted, was baptized and over the years became one of the great saints for the ages.

You have most likely had a time or two where your scripture reading spoke specifically to your current life situation. After serving on both active duty and in the Army Reserves, I retired as Lt. Colonel. I had always thought I'd be promoted to full Colonel, but when it didn't happen I said, "Thank you God, anyway. I'm grateful for what I have."

Later, while retired, I found out that, indeed, I had been recommended to Colonel by a promotion board some ten months before retirement. The next day, when the process was completed and I'd received the promotion letter, I opened my Bible to that day's assigned Scripture reading. It was Psalm 75:6-7, which reads,

> For exaltation comes neither from the east
> Nor from the west nor from the south
> But God is the Judge:
> He puts down one
> And exalts another.

Coincidence? Of course not. God was confirming to me through His word where my promotion came from in this life.

We hear God speak *formally*. This may take place in a sermon, the exposition and preaching of God's word. It may come in the form of a prophetic word to you directly.

When I was a college senior, an old man I did not know prayed for me at the altar of a church where I had just led a program. While praying for me, he spoke to me saying that wherever I served in ministry, "dry bones would come alive." In middle age now I can look back and see how wherever I was, God was indeed bringing life to dry bones.

We may also hear God *informally*. A word or comment may be spoken through a Christian brother or sister that resonates in your soul. A hymn or praise song may have a line or phrase that jumps off the page into your awareness. John Wesley used to say that Methodists would sing their theology. Deep doctrinal truths are especially evident in the great classic hymns. That's why churches become impoverished when they neglect hymns to the partiality of only praise songs. Many contemporary praise songs have wonderful lyrics, but also many sound like "Jesus loves me, this I know. That's why I play my rock and roll."

Listen to God speak through all the themes of reconciliation and redemption.

Of all the hearing aids, God seems to speak *quietly*. "Let us keep our silent sanctuaries," wrote Etienne Senancour, a French writer, "for in them the eternal perspectives are preserved."

When the prophet Elijah was fleeing from King Ahab and Queen Jezebel, discouraged and wanting to die, the word of the Lord came to him, telling him to stand on the mountain before the Lord. A strong wind came by, then an earthquake and a fire, but God was not in those elements. Then came a still, small voice and it was the Lord.[17]

We have to be quieted to hear the still, small voice. We have to be led "beside the still water," as it says in the twenty-third Psalm.[18]

When I've had great decisions to make in my life, I always go to quiet places, especially beside the still water. A lake, an ocean, or a river have all been my silent sanctuaries. I've gone to a monastery. The noises that stain me every day diminish in the quiet places and I begin to hear the still, small voice.

God spoke through Jeremiah saying,

> O you sword of the LORD,
> How long until you are quiet?
> Put yourself up into your scabbard,
> Rest and be still.[19]

The Psalmist admonished us to "Meditate within your heart on your bed, and be still."[20]

In the quiet stillness you become aware of what could be called soul conversation. Deep hearkens unto deep. You receive direction and revelation.

At age twenty three, I was pretty sure I had met the girl of my dreams. I only wanted to do this once and I wanted to do it right, so I set aside two days of quiet, prayer, and fasting where I sought to be spiritually sensitive to hearing God's direction.

Near the end of my two-day quiet soul conversation, I distinctly heard God say, "You may marry Cinda. She is my gift to you." Thus, filled with confidence, we were able to make the second-most-important decision (after salvation) in our young lives.

Finally you may hear God *surprisingly*. A billboard, an advertising jingle on the radio, a commercial or show on television may all be sources for the voice of God to break through if you're alert. It was Jesus who said, "Therefore, take heed *how* you hear."(emphasis added)[21]

Young mothers have demonstrated the ability to focus on other tasks yet remain attentive to the slightest cry or movement of their babies. In the midst of our busy lives, God may still speak to us in a variety of surprising ways that we could never limit by putting them in print.

Some additional thoughts of auditories:
   1) Be especially aware of God speaking through:
      a) casual conversation;
      b) nature;
      c) dreams;
      d) secular songs.

Recently, I heard a testimony of a woman whose ex-husband had threatened to take away her boys. While in the midst of a deep emotional struggle, she was driving in her car and the song lyric, "Don't worry, baby. Everything will turn out alright," came on the radio. She felt it was God's comforting word to her and indeed it was—even through a Beach Boys song!

2) When trying to distinguish God's voice from your own, ask these questions:
    a) Does it bring freedom or bondage?
    b) Does it turn you towards God or away?
    c) Does it lift up (honor) Christ?
    d) Is it in harmony with scripture?
    e) Are people edified (encouraged)?

3) A final great scripture verse to pray in faith, "Now this is the confidence that we have in Him; that if we ask anything according to His will, He hears us."[22]

Amen and Amen.

For we are to God the fragrance of Christ among those who are being saved and among those who are perishing. To the one we are the aroma of death leading to death, and to the other the aroma of life leading to life.

- 2 Corinthians 2:15-16

You are already clean because of the word which I have spoken to you.

- John 15:3

Sleep with clean hands either clean all day by integrity or washed clean at night by repentance.

- John Donne

We do not lose peace with God over another person's sin, but only over our own. Only when we are willing to be cleansed there will we have peace.

- Roy Hession

"What God has cleansed you must not call common."

- Acts 10:15

Just as Jesus found it necessary to sweep the money-changers from the Temple porch, so we ourselves need to do a lot of housecleaning.

- Dale Evans Rogers

The blood of Jesus Christ His Son cleanses us from all sin.

- 1 John 1:7

There is only one way to achieve happiness on this terrestrial ball. And that is to have either a clear conscience or none at all.

- Ogden Nash

Chapter Five
Smell
Spiritual Cleansing

The sense of smell has the connotation of spiritual cleanliness. The olfactory sense is very much an unappreciated ability. Smell is very evocative. Odors give us an uncanny ability to recall the entire ambiance of an event. They can bring to mind a number of senses, including what you saw and heard and even felt at a particular time. For example, the smell of a turkey cooking can bring up memories of Thanksgiving as a child.

Biologists such as 2005 Nobel prize winner Linda Buck have shown how this sense works in human beings. In her research, she discovered that odors are detected in the air by "oderant receptors," which are proteins found in the nose. Human noses have around 350 of these receptors, which detect smells and send coded signals to the brain. There, in the olfactory section of the cortex, is a precise map of receptor signals. This is a map that you maintain your whole life, which is why you can recognize an odor you may not have smelled for years.[1]

The Bible and Christian living have a great deal to do with smell and cleanliness. The smells of the Jewish sacrificial system must have been powerful, evocative reminders of cleansing and forgiveness. As animal flesh burned on the altar, it was a "sweet savor" unto God. The smells of a good stew were enough to make Esau sell his birthright. The smell of the re-enactment of Holy Communion brought forth the thoughts and deep meanings of the Last Supper with Jesus to his followers. Candles burning reminded believers of the presence of the Holy Spirit.

The current popularity of aromatherapy can be traced to the sense of peace and relaxation associated with certain smells. While there are not any cogent studies demonstrating whether it really works, there could be something to it. Studies with mice have shown that exposing them to different odors, elicits different types of behaviors.

Spiritual cleansing has a lot to do with behavior. We note that in scripture there are levels of cleansing behavior. There is an initial cleansing and a continual cleansing. These are necessary because of uncleanliness and spiritual sickness that surround us in a sin-polluted world.

Initial cleansing is like an operation where Christ does a radical surgery in our lives to make us spiritually well. *Continual cleansing* is analogous to caring for these wounds. It is changing the bandages and using antiseptic to keep the germ of sin out so you are deeply healed. And coming to church is like a weekly visit to the hospital where you undergo an examination and are given a prescription for the week.

Initial cleansing and continual cleansing are both parts of a process. When you mow your lawn, you cut the top of the weed and the weed eventually grows back. Initial cleansing is cutting the top of the weeds. Continual cleansing leads to removing most of the roots of the weeds themselves.

Cleanliness Is Next to Godliness

It all starts with the initial cleansing. Jesus lived in a society that was especially concerned with cleanliness. Following laws in Leviticus and Deuteronomy, the Jews had detailed direction on what cleanliness and uncleanliness meant.

Certain foods, such as pigs or rabbits, were avoided. A woman after childbirth was unclean. A person who touched a dead body was ceremonially unclean. Priests had to wash and bathe before leading worship services. On top of these and many more, the rabbis of the day added further rules, laying a heavier burden on the people. Jesus was scandalized because he and the disciples didn't wash their hands in the ritually prescribed way. His revolutionary answer was that uncleanliness had nothing to do with what goes on or in a person. It's what is in a person's heart that defiles him or her. That was the critical nature of cleanliness.[2]

Sin is what makes us unclean. Impure. The word *impurity* is the same root word used for an unclean wound. We are infected by sinful, wrong thoughts and resultant actions.

Today, in Western society, people are seriously examining the decline of civilization and opining as to what could be wrong. Substance abuse, violence, crime, immorality, lack of ethical behavior and civility, and laziness permeate the culture. There is growing moral uncleanliness.

The writer of Proverbs put it clearly: "There is a generation that is pure in its own eyes, yet is not washed from its filthiness."[3]

In New Jersey, an artist is marketing "guilt bags" to relieve "guilt pressure build-up." You blow your guilt into the bag, you pop the bag and presto—the guilt is supposed to be gone. You can purchase ten bags for $2.50 and see if it works. (It doesn't!)

I once counseled a young man who took three baths a day (up to an hour each time) and yet never felt clean. Shakespeare's character Lady Macbeth was famous for washing her hands again and again to relieve the guilt of her actions. The real germs were on the inside and of a sin-nature.

People don't feel clean on the inside. I am told that by clients regularly in counseling sessions. They are not who they appear outwardly.

Oh, but we look clean on the outside! A teacher was checking her student's knowledge of popular proverbs and asked, "Class, cleanliness is next to what?" One small boy answered with real feeling, "Next to impossible?"

You see, Americans interpret outer cleansing with great significance. How we've come to depend upon and love our own shampoos, deodorants, bath soaps, colognes, and perfumes to make us clean outwardly, and yet we're not clean inwardly. We learn as children that cleanliness is next to godliness and then focus on the outer person.

At age twelve, I got ready to go to my first junior-high dance, one of the first baby steps towards the adult world. I scrubbed and lathered myself that evening in preparation for the big event. I spent a good hour in the bathroom:

- I washed and rinsed my hair three times
- I splashed on my dad's Old Spice. (I'd heard good things about Old Spice…and I might even try a slow dance!)
- I covered myself with talcum powder because I wasn't going to have a drop of sweat or body odor on me.

And then my mother knocked on the bathroom door asking if I was okay. She had observed clouds of talcum powder wafting under the doorway to the kitchen. I had learned well to be very clean on the outside…but not on the inside yet.

That's the problem with people in America. Crystal clean bodies outside—unclean inside. We smell fine outwardly—we smell inwardly.

On the outside, we wear the cleanest clothes in the world. We look so neat and clean and pressed!

I always thought I was a fairly clean guy—before I got married. As a bachelor, when I wanted clean clothes I'd just put all my duds in the same wash, with the same water temperature, and then into the same dryer at the same heat level. Some bachelor readers may still wash their clothes in a similar manner. My clothes were relatively clean and I felt OK about them.

Then I got married and came to understand that women had a totally different idea of clean. They follow a complex process involving:

– sorting;
– presoaking;
– twenty-two various combinations of water temperatures;
– stain remover;
– fabric softener;
– cream rinse and ointments (just kidding).

It's like a chemistry experiment—and I didn't do well in chemistry. So, for years I didn't do laundry in our marriage because the few times I tried, it wasn't up to someone's standard. (No names mentioned here.) When I did try doing laundry, someone's blouses came out in a size only Tinkerbell or maybe Britney Spears could wear. The reason was the clothes were supposed to be washed in cold water and dried flat. Instead, I put them in hot water and heavy-dry.

Now I've learned to read the labels! The labels give me instructions for cleaning. God's word gives us clear instructions for cleaning. Check the label. People's lives are often a mess because they don't read the labels. Malachi wrote: "For He is a refiner's fire and like a launderer's soap."[4]

God can clean our inward lives. The blood of Jesus Christ cleanses us from all sin.[5] Normally, we think of blood staining items, but this blood cleans completely. This is the initial cleansing. Isaiah prophesied, saying

> Though your sins are like scarlet,
> They shall be as white as snow;
> Though they are red like crimson,
> They shall be as wool.[6]

"I, even I, am He who blots out your transgressions for My own sake; And I will not remember your sins."[7]

A college student who I had the privilege of leading towards Christ said she felt "like she'd swallowed liquid sunshine." Salvation through Christ cleanses us and then is symbolized in baptism. The powerful display of baptism is such a remarkable symbol of God's cleansing inner work that even sinless Jesus submitted to it.

Once you've experienced being clean, you want to stay that way. That's why we read our Bible, pray, and go to church to stay close to God's word. Jesus said, "You are already clean because of the word which I have spoken to you. Abide in me and I in you."[8]

Can you think of a time when you were really, really dirty, perhaps having done a filthy job and you couldn't wait to scrub up and get clean all over before joining the human race again? I had an entire summer like that. I had landed the best paying job a sixteen year old could get in our town. It was at an onion-ring factory, which smelled terrible.

I would arrive for the 11 p.m. to 7 a.m. shift and all the machines would be whirring and cutting hundreds of onions every minute. You know how onions make your eyes tear up? I would cry for the first fifteen to twenty minutes of each shift, and by the end of eight hours of work, I would be filthy from head to toe and smell absolutely awful.

I'd race home at 7 a.m. and scrub all over in the bath for the longest time. It felt wonderful to be clean, and I'd ask my folks and friends, "Do I smell OK? Do I smell like onions at all?" It was like being reborn each morning.

Spiritually, when God does an initial cleansing, we aren't really used to feeling that way. We wonder and feel guilty and may ask a close friend or our pastor, "Am I doing OK? Am I really cleaned up?" It's difficult for us to believe, since we've spent so long being used to the dirt and stain of sin.

Yet that is exactly what God did for you. Your sins are separated as far as the east is from the west. They are cast into the sea of forgetfulness (for God remembers them no more) and a sign is put up that reads "No fishing allowed!"

Bramlin North, the British evangelist, was on a preaching mission in the midlands of Great Britain. On one night of revival services, he came into the church and was handed a letter—personal, private, sealed. The letter was from a person who'd known him in his pre-Christian days. The pages described one of the most sordid pages in his past and went on to say that if he started to preach tonight, a person would stand up and read a copy of the letter to the congregation.

Bramlin North went up to the pulpit and when it came time for the sermon, he took out the letter and read it. He then went on to declare, "Every word in this letter is true. But you can see

God in Christ has forgiven me, and tonight I want to speak to you about Christ, who can forgive you and deliver you from evil."

Continual Cleansing

When we experience initial cleansing, we become aware of salvation's effect at several levels. This is continual cleansing. Our speech is most clearly impacted. I grew up in a home where coarse language was not allowed. On at least one occasion, I learned the hard way by saying a bad word. I found out that Ivory soap *was* 99 and 44/100 percent pure soap because it was put in my mouth!

I never heard my mother or father swear—even once. But we live in a different culture, where we are surrounded by language that stains and degrades. While even in the midst of "air" pollution, God can guard your tongue and change your speech pattern.

God also cleanses our hands. You can't even approach God without clean hands.

The Psalmist prayed, "Who may ascend into the hill of the LORD or stand in His holy place? He who has clean hands and a pure heart.[9]"

James wrote, "Draw near to God and He will draw near you. Cleanse your hands, you sinners; and purify your hearts, you double-minded."[10]

We remember earlier that Jesus was criticized by the Pharisees for not having clean hands. Hand washing, to the Pharisees, had become a ritual to please God.

Water jars were used before the meals. A devout Jew would have the water first poured on both hands, held with fingers pointed upwards, and would let it run up the arm as far as the wrist. The water had to drop off at the wrist, for the water itself was now unclean, having touched unclean hands and if ran down the fingers again, it would render them unclean.

The process was repeated with hands held in the opposite direction, with fingers pointed down, and then each hand was cleansed by being rubbed with the fist of the other. The very strictest of Jews would do this not only before a meal, but also between each of the courses! Physically clean hands were important and even more so, now.

The American Society for Microbiology studied the handwashing habits of Americans and found some disturbing results.

According to the Associated Press, the researchers hid in stalls or pretended to comb their hair as they observed 6,333 men and women in restrooms in five cities.

The results: In New York's Penn Station only 60 percent of those using restrooms washed up. At a Braves game in Atlanta, 64 percent washed. The study found that women wash their hands more than do men, 74 percent of women washing their hands after using the toilet versus only 61 percent of men.[11]

In 1818, Ignaz Philipp Semmelweis was born into a world of dying women. The finest hospitals lost one out of six young mothers to the scourge of "childbed fever."

A doctor's daily routine began in the dissecting room, where he performed autopsies. From there he made his way to the hospital to examine expectant mothers without ever pausing to wash his hands. Dr. Semmelweis was the first man in history to associate such examinations with the resultant infection and death. His own practice was to wash with a chlorine solution, and after eleven years and the delivery of 8,537 babies, he lost only 184 mothers—about one in fifty.

He spent the vigor of his life lecturing and debating with his colleagues. Once he argued,

> "Puerperal fever is caused by decomposed material conveyed to a wound… I have shown how it can be prevented. I have proved all that I have said. But while we talk, talk, talk, gentlemen, women are dying. I am not asking anything world shaking. I am asking you only to wash…For God's sake, wash your hands."

But virtually no one believed him. Doctors and midwives had been delivering babies for thousands of years without washing, and no outspoken Hungarian was going to change them now! Semmelweis died insane at the age of forty-seven, his wash basins discarded, his colleagues laughing in his face, and the death rattle of a thousand women ringing in his ears.[12]

Are *your* hands clean? Now, we're naturally not referring to dirt, but what your hands do. How long would you go without washing your hands? A few hours? A day or two? And yet people go weeks and months and years with unclean hands before God.

The distinguished pastor of the Brick Presbyterian Church in New York, Dr. Babcock, was approached by a physician, a member of his congregation, who was concerned about his health. Handing Dr. Babcock some theatre tickets he said, "Take these. You need the recreation of going to this play." His pastor looked at them.

Seeing they were tickets to a play of the kind he could not conscientiously attend, he said kindly, "Thank you, but I can't take them. I can't go."

"Why not?" the physician asked.

"Doctor, it's this way. You're a physician; a surgeon, in fact. When you operate, you scrub your hands meticulously until you are especially clean. You wouldn't dare operate with dirty hands. I'm a servant of Christ. I deal with precious human souls. I wouldn't dare to do my service with a dirty life."

Maybe you don't have theatre tickets in your hands, but they do hold the remote control to your television. Your hands can open God's word or a tasteless magazine. Your hands can do needed research on the internet or turn to an inappropriate web site. Your hands can operate your wallet to do the Lord's work or to keep a death-grip on your precious possessions.

God can clean your hands. God will also cleanse what you listen to and watch. Isaiah admonishes, "Wash yourselves, make yourselves clean; Put away the evil of your doings from before My eyes."[13]

Christians practice the holy habits of scripture reading and attending church to be cleansed by God's word. There is great value in this practice.

The British weekly published this provocative letter:

Dear editor,
It seems ministers feel their sermons are very important and spend a great deal of time preparing for them. I have been attending church quite regularly for thirty years and I have probably heard 3,000 of them. To my consternation, I discovered I cannot remember a single sermon. I wonder if a minister's time might be more profitably spent on something else?

For weeks a storm of editorial responses ensued… finally ended by this letter:

Dear editor,
I have been married for 30 years. During that time, I have eaten 32,850 meals—mostly my wife's cooking. Suddenly I have discovered I cannot remember the menu of a single meal. And yet, I have the distinct impression that without them, I would have starved to death long ago.

God's word feeds and cleanses our soul, which leads us to the heart of continual cleansing. Only Christ can reach deep within your very soul and cleanse within. Jay Johns, now a British evangelist, was converted to Christ as a college student. When he came home during the break, he told his mother he'd become a believer in God. His mother, fearing Jay had gotten caught up in a cult, exclaimed, "You've been brainwashed!"

Jay replied, "Oh, yes, mother. I've been brainwashed. My brain has been washed clean by God. And mother, if you knew what was in my brain before I met Jesus, you'd be glad my brain was washed."

The Smell of Success

Here is something interesting about smell as a spiritual sense. The physical sense of smell decreases as we age, and that can diminish life's quality because we can't enjoy the scents around us and the flavor of foods. This is not so with the spiritual sense of cleanliness. If anything, it becomes stronger with age. As one walks closer to the refiner's fire, it grows, for our God is a consuming fire.[14] The Holy Spirit cleanses our very consciences from dead works so we can serve the living God.[15]

If there is a key to success in this process, it appears to be obedience. I heard someone say once that if you do something for God and don't feel like it, you're a hypocrite. I would suggest that is blatantly untrue. If you do something you've got to do and don't feel like it, *yet you do it,* you've got character! You'll never grow in spiritual cleanliness if you just live by your feelings.

Let me ask you, if you were God, which of the following scenarios would cause you to appreciate me more?

I was obedient one day and I felt like it and it was easy to be obedient. The next day I didn't feel like being obedient and it was hard for me, yet I was obedient anyway.

Which would cause you to appreciate me more?

Of course it's doing the right thing regardless of feelings. The fruit of the Spirit grows in the garden of obedience. Where he leads, I will follow; what he feeds, I will swallow.

The Apostle Paul wrote,

> Therefore, having these promises, beloved, let us cleanse ourselves from all filthiness of the flesh and spirit, perfecting holiness in the fear of God.[16]

This is radical obedience. Dr. Donald Gary Barnhouse once told of a missionary home in the Congo where the little son was playing alone in the yard. Suddenly, he heard his father's voice. "Philip, obey me instantly. Drop to your stomach!" The boy obeyed without asking a question. "Now crawl to me as fast as you can!" Again, the boy obeyed. "Now stand up and run to me!" Philip got up and ran into his father's arms. Only then did he turn to look back at the tree under which he had been playing. Hanging from the lower tree limb was a fifteen-foot venomous snake.

Suppose Philip had stopped to ask, "Why, Dad?" or "Do I have to do it right now?" as many small children would have asked. He then would have been killed instantly by the snake. Instant obedience becomes a mark of those who smell success in Christian living.

Christians must also be willing to face themselves as they clean out their spiritual houses. Ray Stedman once referred to a school teacher who was a member of his congregation. She had taught school for twenty-five years. When she heard of a job that meant a promotion, she applied for the position. When someone else was hired, the school teacher protested to the principal about her many years of experience. The principal responded, "I'm sorry, but you haven't had the twenty-five years of experience as you claim: you've had one year's experience twenty-five times."

Christians must courageously clean out their spiritual houses. Some of us make the same errors and cave in to the same sins year after year, allowing odorous sin to accumulate in our lives. We can be Christians for twenty-five years, but with only one year's experience practiced twenty-five times. We are still "babes in Christ."

Dennis DeHaan once described a rubber plant he had purchased for his wife. It was a beautiful plant with large, luxurious leaves. One morning he noticed all its leaves were drooping as if dejected. He didn't say anything to his wife and when he came home at noon, the plant looked completely transformed. It looked as healthy as the day he got it at the store. The leaves had a healthy color and were extended out again and it smelled good.

Dennis asked his wife about it and she told him she'd been reading a household hint book which contained some suggestions for keeping plants looking alive and fresh. The book said dust accumulated on the leaves actually prevent light from getting to them. Therefore, it's necessary to regularly wipe them clean. She had done this with her plant and the results were evident.

Particles of sin can "dust" our lives and build up. Resentments, sharp words, unforgiveness, impure thoughts, or selfish attitudes all take their toll on our spirituality and an eventual layer can cover us and prevent mercy and grace from entering in.

I was on a flight from Los Angeles to Phoenix and the man who sat next to me began detailing the problems in his life. I don't wear a clerical collar, nor tell people outright that I'm a clergyman and a counselor, but they seem to sense and smell the savor of God's presence in me.

Within minutes, the man was telling me how his wife had been flirtatious with other men and it made him so angry and jealous. He just couldn't get over the indiscretions and he wouldn't talk to his wife about it. He just held it in, and over time an unclean layer of dust had accumulated in his spiritual house.

One day, he was eating in a Chinese restaurant and some food got stuck in his throat. Eventually it went down, but it was a frightening experience.

For the next six weeks, his throat was so swollen he could barely drink water. Though the throat had been very mildly traumatized by the temporarily stuck food, the doctors could find nothing wrong with his throat. One night he talked things out with his wife. She apologized and he forgave her. The next morning he awoke with his throat just fine.

It wasn't only the Chinese food that caused his throat to swell. It was quite literally the anger and unforgiveness—the words stuck in his throat. When he cleared his throat through forgiveness, he was well again.

Wait, There's More

There's one final element of cleansing that is most critical to our spiritual growth. The truth is, for all our best efforts, we can never fully cleanse ourselves utilizing our own good intentions. Great saints of God have recognized this deficiency in themselves. Many terms have been used, such as

- Baptism in the Holy Spirit;
- Full salvation;
- Holiness;
- Sanctification; and
- Growth in grace.

It doesn't really matter what you call it. It is pursuing a holy life and expecting God to work by faith.

Let me give an example. Have you ever been in church, perhaps on a regular basis, and you really didn't feel a part of it? You were in the church, but the church wasn't in you. Your mind was out there somewhere. You weren't particularly spiritually sensitive. You're a Christian, but your subconscious mind keeps bringing in impure or distracting thoughts into your conscious awareness.

E. Stanley Jones helps our thinking here:

> Perhaps it can best be described in more understandable terms as the "unconverted subconscious." The subconscious is like the submerged portion of an iceberg, one tenth above and nine tenths below. Freud says we are determined by lower drives in the subconscious. We think we consciously determine our conduct but those basic drives in the subconscious actually determine us.[17]

These basic drives in the subconscious can be described as self, sex, and the herd. When you gave yourself to Christ you gave everything that was in your awareness. That would be your conscious mind. Yet there below lies nine tenths of you, your subconscious, still unsurrendered to God. In moments of your life, I bet at times you are very well aware of this "lower nature."

Let's not just quote Freud. The Apostle Paul used similar language in his letter to the Galatians:

> I say then: Walk in the Spirit, and you shall not fulfill the lust of the flesh. For the flesh lusts against the Spirit, and the Spirit against the flesh; and these are contrary to one another, so that you do not do the things that you wish.[18]

Some versions translate the flesh as "the lower nature," consistent with our thoughts or our subconscious. You can relate to this. You want to do something right. In fact, you will to do it. And then there is this real conflict, an inner war that erupts. Either the lower nature wins out or your new Spirit-controlled nature is the victor.

It is obvious that Christians do have these struggles. Skevington Woods notes, "It is the recognition that believers are at once redeemed from sin and yet not out of its grip."[19]

Wesley recognized this helplessness that

> "they are no more able to know of themselves to think one good thought, to form one good desire, to speak one good word, or to do one good work, then before they were justified."[20]

What this work of the Spirit does is gives you victory even over the subconscious mind. It cleanses you throughout. You can't get rid of the basic drives of self, sex, and the herd, for they are a part of you. The Spirit can monitor control over them and redirect them for kingdom purposes. E. Stanley Jones assists our thinking once again:

> So we say with the coming of the Holy Spirit both the conscious and the subconscious minds are cleansed from sin and evil bents. So instead of sitting on a lid in suppression, you now take off the lid and bid those urges, now emancipated, to go forth and love and serve in the name and power of their Master and Lord.[21]

At age nineteen, I realized this truth and quietly, by faith, asked God to fill me with the Holy Spirit to cleanse me and give me the resurrection power I needed to live the clean life I'd always wanted. God graciously granted it so that my life could be a sweet savor to God. Do you have it? Or better yet, does the Spirit have you? You will know if you have the power.

Some additional thoughts for the Sense of Smell and Cleanliness

1) The Bible distinguishes between "weights" and "sin." A weight obviously slows you down in life but is not a sin. Be aware of habits or practices that may not be sins but over time could start to steer you away to unclean practices.

2) A good question from Gestalt counseling is "Where is there deadness in your life?" Be aware of where deadness lurks and causes the perfume of your life to be overcome.

3) Go through the Bible and see how often the issue of cleanliness comes up. It's important on God's agenda!

Too much of our orthodoxy is correct and sound, but like words without a tune, it does not glow and burn; it does not stir the heart; it has lost its hallelujah. One man with a genuine glowing experience with God is worth a library full of arguments.

- Vance Havner

We are all the time following the influences which will presently be our rulers; we are making our own destiny. We are choosing our habits, our associates, our traits, our homes. In time these acquire a power over us which enslaves our will, and from them we neither will nor can break loose.

- Herman Wayland

What a mistake to suppose that the passions are strongest in youth! The passions are not stronger, but the control over them is weaker! They are more easily excited, they are more violent and apparent; but they have less energy, less durability, less intense and concentrated power than in mature life.

- Edward George Bulwer-Lytton

God makes his ministers a flame of fire. Am I ignitable? God, deliver me from the dread of asbestos of "other things." Saturate me with the oil of thy Spirit that I may be a flame. Make me thy fuel, Flame of God.

- Jim Elliot

The happiness of a man in this life does not consist in the absence but in the mastery of his passions.

- Alfred Tennyson

His delight is in the law of the LORD, and is His law he meditates day and night.

- Psalm 1:2

"A holy life does not live in the closet," wrote E. M. Bounds, "but it cannot live without the closet."

Chapter Six
Taste
Spiritual Appetite

The sense of taste is like spiritual appetite. If you go to a physician, you will be asked to stick out your tongue so it can be examined. The doctor can tell a lot about your health just by looking at your tongue. There is a corresponding truth in the spiritual realm.

Just as a physical connection exists between smell and taste, so there is a relationship between spiritual cleansing and appetite. When you have been cleansed, your appetites begin to change. And, most importantly, your appetites reflect your interests. Your interests display your spiritual health.

It is likely that you have participated in a service of Holy Communion before. The smell of the wine or grape juice and the taste of it along with the bread evokes sensory memories of similar events. It reminds you of the cleansing work of Christ and the forgiveness that comes through his shed blood. When the Emmaus disciples met the risen Christ, they didn't recognize him at first. But when Jesus blessed and broke the bread in their presence, their eyes were opened, their hearts burned within them and they were compelled to tell others.[1] Their greater appetite was for the things of God.

The Bible itself says a great deal about eating and drinking. It begins with eating from a fruit tree in Genesis 3 and ends with a fruit tree and drinking from the water of life in the Revelation of John.[2] However, as is often true in scripture, many narrative references speak to more than just the physical nature of food and our appetites.

Examples from scripture include:
- Taste and see that the LORD is good.³
- "My food is to do the will of Him who sent Me, and to finish His work."⁴
- And Jesus said to them, "I am the bread of life. He who comes to Me shall never hunger, and he who believes in Me shall never thirst.⁵
- "To him who overcomes I will give to eat from the tree of life which is in the midst of the Paradise of God."⁶
- To him who overcomes I will give some of the hidden manna to eat.⁷

Our appetites *do* reveal our interests. The closer we walk with Christ over the years, the more we develop a voracity for the things of God. Taste involves experiencing God. When you taste the life of God and drink from living water, "pleasures for a season" pale in comparison.

Lining up in a frozen yogurt shop, I had time to observe how several people in front of me made their orders. Some knew exactly what they wanted. They immediately ordered a flavor or a blend with nuts. They had tasted it before and it was good.

Others, though, had to try little spoon samples. These customers would taste it, roll their eyes around, and then make a selection.

I see many Christians in the latter group. They've tasted and seen that the Lord is good, but they keep experimenting with other flavors. The world is just too colorful, pleasurable, and attractive. A craving, an addiction, or a need overtakes and supersedes one's spiritual appetite for the things of God.

In Greek mythology, King Tantalus offended the gods and was punished in the underworld. He was placed in a lake in water up to his chin, but whenever he attempted to satisfy his burning thirst the water receded. Over his head were branches laden with choice fruit, but when he tried to satisfy his hunger they eluded his grasping hands. Tantalus, therefore, became the symbol of utter frustration. Even today his name is remembered in the English word *tantalize*.

It is possible to take nearly anything in this wonderful world God has created, pervert it, and develop such a desire for it that it will corrupt your soul. You see it throughout the scriptural narrative.

Adam and Eve had all the remarkable pleasures of Eden at their disposal. That was not enough, though. They didn't eat of the tree of the knowledge of good and evil because it looked tasty. The real issue was a craving for independence and power, which, given full rein, caused awful consequences.

In the Genesis 25 story of Jacob and Esau, you read of Esau coming home famished from a hunting trip. He can't think of anything except the gnawing hunger in his stomach. Jacob offers him immediate gratification- a meal in exchange for a birthright. This was not an issue of food. It is being so concerned with immediate needs you sacrifice your very inheritance.

It is indeed possible, as the Apostle Paul has written, that "those who are such do not serve our Lord Jesus Christ, but their own belly."[8] I know a lot of people who are like this. It was Paul Tillich who commented that your ultimate concern is actually your god. That's god with a small g.

For example, like Esau, a man could become so wrapped up in hunting and fishing (or any other sport) that he neglects his very family and inheritance. Listen to guy conversations and how sports can dominate the interchange. It has become a god. An appetite can cause you to neglect and lose your birthright.

I worked for eighteen months in a Veteran's Administration hospital, where, on nearly a daily basis, I assisted in the alcohol rehabilitation program. This five-week, in-residence program was for men whose lives had been all but destroyed because of a single appetite for beverage alcohol. I met some of the finest men I've known in that setting. These were good, often honorable, respectable, and successful men who sold their birthrights for a beverage. Their appetites went out of control and became addictions. Craig Brian Larson comments on the condition of addiction in a larger context:

A novel by Madeleine L'Engle is entitled A Severed Wasp. The title, which comes from one of George Orwell's essays, offers a graphic image of human lostness.

Orwell describes a wasp that "was sucking jam on my plate and I cut him in half. He paid no attention, merely went on with his meal, while a tiny stream of jam trickled out of his severed esophagus. Only when he tried to fly away did he grasp the dreadful thing that had happened to him."

The wasp and people without Christ have much in common. Severed from their souls, but greedy and unaware, people continue to consume life's sweetness. Only when it's time to fly away will they grasp their dreadful condition.[9]

The progression of addicted tastes was made evident in the subtle lure of advertisement. Note the order in ads for the beer Michelob over the years:
- Holidays were made for Michelob;
- Weekends were made for Michelob;
- Put a little weekend in your week with Michelob;
- The nights belong to Michelob.

What's next? Michelob in the morning? Your life belongs to Michelob? Mask your pain with Michelob? Talk about a sequence of sin!

And so we turn to the sin-destroyer. *Through* Christ we have our tastes and passions restricted. It is *from* Christ we see how to go about this.

It especially appears that our appetites in early adulthood often tug us away from the very purposes of God for our lives. While we'll cover spiritual strength in a later chapter, we note that at the start of Jesus' public ministry he goes into the wilderness to fast and pray and there faces the pull of appetites by the tempter. In all my years of working with young adults on college campuses, I see the very same patterns and strategy to derail precious promising people from the fullness of their life calling. There are three in number employed by the evil one: needs, respect or honor, and attention or acclaim.[10]

Needs

The tempter encouraged Jesus to turn stones into bread. No doubt Jesus was hungry after many days of a supernatural fast. Now there's nothing wrong with doing miraculous things with bread. Jesus would feed 4,000 and 5,000 people with wonder bread and fishes. It just wasn't the time for this display of meeting of physical needs.

Jesus' answer was that man does not live by bread alone but by every word of God. He recognized there were greater spiritual appetites. If you direct your gaze heavenward, you experience a concurrent uplifting of your passions to God.

All of us have great difficulty resisting the pull downward to gazing horizontally rather than vertically. We find ourself enveloped by life concerns and everyday needs. When these needs are not met well, we may feel powerless.

We find ourselves thinking "Oh, if I could only win the lottery!" And yet, 80 percent of lottery winners spend it all within forty-eight months. Or we say "if I could just be a famous athlete with money and prowess!" And yet, 75 percent of all NBA players go broke within five years.

Maturity is understanding that God will take care of your most basic needs. When you have grasped God's timing for turning stones into bread and when you fully comprehend you don't live by bread alone, you're ready to spiritually move up.

It was Abraham Maslow who posited a hierarchy of needs. This fundamental order of how humans seem to operate can be answered in the spiritual realm as well. Maslow said the needs went in this order from bottom to top:

Self Actualization
Self Esteem
Love and Belongingness
Safety Needs
Physical Needs

To a great degree, the first four levels of needs are self-centered.

Before we can reach self-actualization, a form of highest potential and a life of altruism, we have to make significant progress step by step through the previous stages. Physical and personal needs must be met at a satisfactory level to grow out of a needs-based existence to a life of giving.

Spiritually, each of these needs can be answered by Scriptural principles:

Physical Needs	But seek first the kingdom of God and His righteousness, and all these things shall be added to you. (Matthew 6:33)
Safety Needs	Be anxious for nothing, but in everything by prayer and supplication, with thanksgiving, let your requests be made known to God; and the peace of God, which surpasses all understanding, will guard your hearts and minds through Christ Jesus. (Philippians 4:6-7)
Love and Belongingness	Who shall separate us from the love of Christ? ...For I am persuaded that neither death nor life, nor angels nor principalities nor powers, nor things present nor things to come, nor height nor depth, nor any other created thing, shall be able to separate us from the love of God which is in Christ Jesus our Lord.(Romans 8:35, 38-39)
Self Esteem and Self Actualization	And be renewed in the spirit of your mind, and that you put on the new man which was created according to God, in true righteousness and holiness. (Ephesians 4:23-24)

God has promised to "supply all your needs according to His riches in glory by Jesus Christ."[11] Don't be diverted by consuming needs.

Respect or Honor

The tempter then took Jesus to a high mountain, showing Him all the kingdoms of the world in a moment of time. Satan (falsely) indicated to Jesus that if he'd worship him, all the power and glory and authority would be then given to the Christ. Jesus knew immediately it was God alone who is worthy of worship and service. He told the tempter to get to the back of the line where he belonged ("Get behind me, Satan!").

I'm originally writing this as the United States approaches yet another Memorial Day weekend. It is a time of remembering and paying our respects to loved ones who have gone on before us. We go out to gravesites and honor the dead.

Someday, it will be you—and me. It will be our gravesites that will be visited. And will we be worthy of respect?

Robert Schuller believes that deep within every human being is a great hunger for dignity and self respect, and I agree with him. How does one gain that sense?

Earlier in the book I mentioned a phrase I've heard for years, particularly among young men and especially young athletes. It is the statement, "Don't dis me." It is as if to say, "Don't you dare be disrespectful of me! I'm worthy of respect because I've got game. Respect me because I can dribble a basketball or throw a football or act or dance or sing or wear flashy jewelry or know how to trash talk. So… don't dis me!"

Of course, these are all caricatures of misguided young people seeking for something far deeper. Their appetites have been re-directed in young adulthood, and anger ensues when, inevitably, respect does not come.

I understand the need of these young men. As a teenager, I thought if I could just exercise enough, chisel my body, gain a v-shape and 6-pack abs, get a letter jacket, and be good enough in sports, perhaps then I'd have respect.

When that saga ended, I knew if I drove the right car, I'd gain respect. So I bought a souped-up "testosterone-mobile" ('67 Mustang) with flashy colors and wide tires. If you didn't see me coming, you could hear me. The problem with these externals is there's always another rung on the ladder. When I went into the army as an eighteen-year-old, the next rung was earning those coveted sergeant stripes. Over time it became a desire to become an officer. Finally, I became a colonel. And it's never high enough, I'm sure, not even for generals.

Maybe you could throw your life into academics and earn a doctorate. One of my students said Ph.D. should stand for "pretty heavy dude." Or, you could write books. Been there, done that. Where does it end? Answer: *it doesn't*. All of these efforts miss the point of what biblical respect involves. The word *respect* is mentioned many times in scripture. While English speakers associate respect with regard or esteem, respect in the Biblical languages is concerned with being partial to others.

When in Acts 10:34, Paul writes, "God is no respecter of persons," it means God plays no favorites. When you begin to grasp who you are in relation to God, when you respect who God is, ungodly pride begins to die within you. The fear of the Lord, a healthy fear, injects wisdom within your life's paradigm.

Without this attitude, you'll think too highly of yourself. You'll place too much value on your talents, abilities, and own cleverness. You'll spend a lifetime trying to earn respect from human beings—and not from God.

The second chapter of Philippians is often called the great "self-emptying" passage about Jesus:

> Let this mind be in you which was also in Christ Jesus, who, being in the form of God, did not consider it robbery to be equal with God, but made Himself of no reputation, taking the form of a bondservant, and coming in the likeness of men. And being found in appearance as a man, He humbled Himself and became obedient to the point of death, even the death of the cross. Therefore God has also highly exalted Him and given Him the name which is above every name, that at the name of Jesus every knee shall bow, of those in heaven, and of those on earth, and of those under the earth, and that every

tongue should confess that Jesus Christ is Lord, to the glory of God the Father.[12]

There's our example. We see it in the life of Jesus. We don't look to gain respect. We give it away.

One day, George Washington was replacing some stones that a member of his riding party had knocked off a stone fence. Someone remarked, "General, you're too big a man to be doing that!" Looking at what he'd done, Washington replied, "O no, I'm just the right size."

Whoever humbles himself will be exalted. Whoever exalts himself eventually shall be humbled. And it goes deeper than that. Expect disrespect from the world. Sometimes you will be "dissed."

You see I happen to be in the tribe of Christendom called "Method-dissed" (Methodist). Two-hundred-and-fifty years ago, the term *Methodist* was a disrespectful nickname put upon followers of Christ led by an Englishman named John Wesley. They practiced methodical disciplines of Christian living and were mocked for it.

It comes with the package. Paul wrote to the Corinthians,

> For we have been made a spectacle to the world, both to angels and to men. We are fools for Christ's sake, but you are wise in Christ. We are weak, but you are strong. You are distinguished, but we are dishonored.[13]

Paul then shows us how to act:
    Being reviled…we bless.
    Being persecuted…we endure.
    Being defamed…we entreat.

In the temptation, the Holy Spirit gave Jesus the strength to rise above the desperate need for respect. Are you yourself able to be a fool for Christ if that is asked of you? Can you bless those who curse you? Answer kindly when slandered? If you cannot, then you may pride yourself too much and not respect God enough.

Dr. Sara Lightfoot-Lawrence is an African-American professor who teaches at Harvard. Her book, *Respect, An Exploration,* describes how she was born to two remarkable parents in pre-World War II Mississippi. Her father had a Ph.D. in sociology and her mother was a psychiatrist. The family was consistently subjected to denigrating remarks and slights, discrimination and racism, and forced to use back doors to banks and restaurants and drink from "colored" water fountains.

Yet they carried themselves with great dignity and caring. At her father's funeral in 1986, she realized his secret: her father gained respect by giving it away. He talked and listened to the ten year old who shined his shoes in the same manner in which he conversed with a bishop or the college president. He showed great honor and interest to any person in his presence. When you offer it to others, eventually it makes its way back to you.

Attention and Acclaim

The final ploy of Satan was to have Jesus do something spectacular. He encouraged Jesus to leap off the temple, the most visible location in the city, and let the angels catch him. Everyone would notice and "ooh and ah" over him.

Attention. What is it about the lure of wanting to be noticed? A small child on a playground goes down a slide shouting, "Look at me, Mommy." A teenager puts enough piercings in his face and body to resemble a tackle box. Adults overextend their finances so they can dwell in the expensive subdivision. This is a hard appetite to conquer.

I live in Kentucky, where basketball is the other major religion in the state. March madness strikes with an epidemic reach. Some get so caught up in the games on television that when their bowl runs out of popcorn, they don't get up, they just reach under the seat cushions of the sofa and pull out their own homemade trail mix. A surprise in every handful. (Just kidding!)

I did play basketball at one time in my life in front of crowds. I was fortunate enough to be captain of the team one year. Before every game, we'd be in the locker room waiting until the crowds and cheerleaders would begin calling out

"Cameron Comets, where are you?"

"Cameron Comets, where are you?"

Finally, as tension mounted, I would get to lead the team out of the locker room, burst through a paper hoop, and, with the crowd still cheering, usually go on to lose the game. But it was great to have the attention of a crowd, albeit as briefly as a passing comet overhead.

Jesus would later receive this kind of acclaim and attention years after his temptation. In what is called his triumphant entry into Jerusalem, a raucous, cheering crowd shouted, "Jesus Christ, where are you?" This was the original March madness.

But Jesus did not give himself to the clamoring multitude. He knew those who were cheering him would in days be jeering him. Spectacular attention and acclaim is always fleeting. There's always a new front-page headline for tomorrow.

Correctly Directed Appetites

It really is possible for God to redirect your spiritual appetites so there is an alignment with kingdom purposes and passions. When we are told to "taste the Lord and see He is good," it doesn't say it is always tasty. A balanced diet rarely is so. There's sweet and sour. Vegetables along with the dessert.

Perhaps some of you have altered your physical diet in recent years. A friend of mine had a heart bypass operation. His regular breakfast for many years had been two eggs, sausage, and whole milk. His physician told him, "Go ahead and make that sausage for breakfast each morning. Fry it real well, but be sure to take the sausage out of the pan, and use a paper towel to soak up all the grease out of it. Then drop the paper towel into garbage. Finally, take the sausage and do the same thing with it!"

If we can change our diet for health reasons, we can adapt our "soul food" for a nourished interior life. We can't do it on our own strength, as few of us have the willpower to diet on our own. What might these involve?

Focused Prayer. The Psalmist regularly prayed for God to direct his heart, the seat of his passion and volition. Pray specifically for this heart willingness.

Train Instead of Trying. We can learn to master our passions. Saint Francis referred to his body as "Brother Ass," like a stubborn mule. If we simply try and keep doing what we've been doing, we'll keep getting what we've been getting. Training means intentionally developing practices and habits that will cultivate spiritual appetite.

Fellowship. The old log out of the fire illustration fits here. When a log is in the fire with other logs, it ignites as well. Out of the fire, the log quickly loses its flame, diminishes to glowing embers, and finally becomes cold. Your right passions and appetites can be ignited by spending time with others of like mind.

General Westmoreland was reviewing a company of airborne qualified soldiers. He asked one man in the company, "Son, do you like to jump?"

"Yes, sir!" was the immediate reply.

Down the line, he asked another young sergeant if he liked to jump.

"No, sir!" he answered.

"Well, why are you in an airborne ranger unit?" the general asked.

"Sir, I love to be with people who jump!" was the soldier's answer. You want to soar? Be with people who share the same passion.

Seek the Spirit. The Holy Spirit, *the paraclete*, will "come alongside of you" in your moments of struggle. This is what *the paraclete* means. The Spirit is your ally to empower, teach, and guide you in the process. It is God's will that the appetites of your life are aligned with kingdom priorities.

Some additional thoughts

1) Dallas Willard's *The Renovation of the Heart* is a superb resource in this area.

2) Don't be discouraged by the immensity of the task. Failure is not sin. Faithlessness is. Have faith that, like a loving parent, God is training you and directing your passions to be aligned with Christ.

3) Spend time in the gospels and look at the passions and interests of Jesus Christ.

Tell me how much you know of the sufferings of your fellow men and I will tell you how much you have loved them.

- Helmut Thielicke

In the pure, strong hours of the morning, when the soul of the day is at its best, lean upon the window sill of God and look into his face and get the orders for the day. Then go out into the day with the sense of a Hand upon your shoulder and not a chip.

- E. Stanley Jones

> If any lift of mine may ease
> The burden of another,
> God give me love and care and strength
> To help my ailing brother.

- Anonymous

Faith without ethical consequences is a lie. God does not need our sacrifices but he has, nevertheless, appointed a representative to receive them, namely our neighbor. The neighbor always represents the invisible Christ.

- J. S. Whale

Let me never fancy that I have zeal until my heart overflows with love to every human being.

- Henry Martyn

When Heine stood before the great statue of Venus de Milo he exclaimed, "But oh! What was it worth? For she has no arms, the goddess, no hands to reach out and help poor beaten souls like me!"

You can give without loving, but you cannot love without giving.

- Amy Carmichael

The greatest sense in our body is the touch sense. We feel, we love and hate, are touchy and touched, through the touch corpuscles of the skin.

- J. Lionel Taylor

Chapter Seven
Touch Ministry

The sense of touch represents ministry. It's sometimes referred to as *tactile*, relating to or perceptible through touch. Another term is *kinesthetic* which is described as, "A sense mediated by nervous elements in muscles, tendons, and joints and stimulated by bodily movements and tensions."[1]

The general idea is your body in motion. To grow in this spiritual sense is to better understand your kinesthetic response to being in God's presence and to further expend your body's energy in others lives for kingdom purposes.

Your Body—Touched by God

While writing this, I am looking at my hands, which represent ministry. Hands can be employed for useful purposes or destructive activities. Hands can help and heal. I can educate my hands to play an instrument. I may use my hands to write a book that will help people be more sensitive to God. Twenty-three percent of our body's sensory receptors are in our hands.

Rabbi Daniel Lapin explains the significance of hands through the Hebrew word for child, *VeLeD*.

This word is made up of the two letters Y and D with the letter L inserted between them. Now, the letters YD spell another Hebrew words, *hand*. And the letter L, pronounced *lamed*, possesses its own meaning "teach or learn."

Placing this *lamed* (teach or learn) inside the word for hand explains an essence of the word *child*. In one way, a child is similar to a hand that has been programmed or taught what to do. In what way is a child an educated hand? The hand is the organ we chiefly use to convey the things we either need or desire from the world to our body. Whether food, drink, book, or our paycheck, almost everything we acquire comes to us through the agency of our hands.

Many of the phrases we use in English—as well as in many other tongues—confirm our understanding of the hand as a symbol of reaching into the world around us. These phrases include "hand it to me," "it came into my hands," "I have the papers in hand," "lend me a hand," "and give them a handout."[2]

Hands obviously don't have to be applied to all good purposes. Tony Campolo said when he was a child attending Sunday school, he learned the song, "O, be careful little hands what you do." The song stuck in his head, even into the teenage years. He'd be out on a hot date and then that song would enter intrusively into his mind, "O, be careful little hands what you do…"

Body Language

To a degree, our entire bodies tell on us. We are not our bodies alone, but we, as spirit beings, live inside them for this pilgrimage on Earth. Whether we have been touched in positive ways ourselves will, over time, show up in our bodies.

Gestalt therapists helped popularize the term *body language*. Gestalt can refer to a pattern or to the whole. In therapy, these counselors spend quality time observing how your whole body language reflects what you have gone through. Sometimes this is called an *idiomotor response*.

I was at a marriage conference once where the Gestalt therapist leading the workshop had all the couples form a large circle. He then selected a volunteer couple to stand in the center while he simply observed them. The therapist walked around them for about a minute and then opined to the wife, "You're the dominant one in the relationship, aren't you?" A bit startled, the couple looked at each other and then nodded affirmatively to the therapist.

I saw it in an instance. The wife stood stiffly at attention as if she'd left a coat hanger in her jacket. The husband, a successful clergyman, stood stoop-shouldered next to her. Twenty-five years of marriage together, and the relationship was reflected in the idiomotor response.

Once, Abraham Lincoln turned down a recommendation for a cabinet post because he didn't like the man's face. When his staff sputtered that the man couldn't help having his face, Lincoln replied, "Every man over forty is responsible for his own face."

Touch

Bodies tell on us. We own a large Maine Coon cat named Figaro, whom we purchased and adopted into the family when he was just six weeks old. By getting him so early, he bonded with us in a way unlike any animal we've ever owned. His idiomotor response to our touch and affirmation is to prefer to be in our laps (our first laptop!) and purr loudly. Philip Yancey and Paul Brand point out how this occurs:

> Anthropologist Ashley Montagu reported on these and many other similar experiences in his elegant and seminal book Touching. He found close physical contact with a mother animal to be essential to the normal development of young animals. Except for man, all mammals spend great amounts of time licking their young. Animals will often die if they are not licked after birth; they never learn to eliminate waste as one consequence. Montagu concludes that the licking is not for cleanliness, but for essential tactile stimulation.[3]

We as human beings truly need touch to develop well as persons. This begins even after birth as Yancey and Brand further demonstrate:

> Although the role of tactile stimulation during birth remains speculative, the need for touching after birth has been dramatically, and tragically, demonstrated. As late as 1920, the death rate among infants in some foundling hospitals in America approached 100 percent. Then Dr. Fritz Talbot of Boston brought from Germany an unscientific-sounding con-

cept of "tender loving care." While visiting the Children's Clinic in Dusseldorf, he noticed an old woman wandering through the hospital, always balancing a sickly baby on her hip. "That," said his guide, "is Old Anna. When we have done everything for a baby and it still is not doing well, we turn it over to Old Anna, and she cures it."

When Talbot proposed this quaint idea to American institutions, administrations derided the notion that something as archaic as simple touching could improve their care. Statistics soon convinced them. In Bellevue Hospital in New York, after a rule was established that all babies must be picked up, carried around, and "mothered" several times a day, the infant mortality rate dropped from 35 percent to less than 10 percent.[4]

We were obviously made to be touched. We are all sensory creatures. The medium of skin, which ranks highest of all the sense organs, still pales in comparison to the soul's need to be "touched by God."

Spiritual Idiomotor Response

Our bodies are receptors for the grace of God. There is another level of awareness of God's presence, which only could be described as extrasensory. Mystics and saints have written about "knowing," a confident realization of something not revealed through pure physical sense.

We note these connections already on a bonded human level. Twin studies often display an uncanny connection, even across many miles, where twins may be reading the identical book, purchasing similar clothes, thinking exact thoughts or planning similar activities, unaware that the other is doing the very same. Husbands and wives may turn to each other in the moment to bring up the same topic. It is a uniting and blendedness where the "two become one." Much like the elderly couple at dinner who had been married for sixty years. The husband turned to the wife and asked, "Which one of us doesn't like broccoli?"

Mothers and their children often have this remarkable affiliation. When my wife, Cinda, was pregnant with our second child, she "knew" it was a girl. We did no ultrasound nor amniotic fluid test because she was so certain God heard our prayer for a healthy little girl. Baby showers requests were only for pink items. Everything in the nursery was readied for a female. And, of course, it was our beautiful daughter, Eva.

That special connection still exists. When Eva was in junior high, Cinda dropped her off at the high school in the early evening for dance team practice. It was twilight and getting dark fast. It looked lonely and nearly deserted except for a couple workmen walking into the building, but this is where she understood the practice would be held. Cinda drove off and when just a little over a mile away, a "knowing" struck her with great clarity. Eva was alone and afraid and trying to call her on a pay phone. (This was before cell phones were in vogue). The practice wasn't at that location at all.

Cinda immediately recognized it as being from God and turned her car around in the road and dashed back to the school to see Eva inside the school's glass doors, hanging up the phone. Indeed, everything she had perceived in her spirit was totally accurate.

Since your body and soul have an inter-relatedness, there is a natural physical response to God. It can be to God's *presence*. In the Bible, you see characters like Daniel, Isaiah, and Peter kneel or fall down in response to the manifestation of God. Perhaps you have been at a worship service where during the time of praise and adoration you felt your body swaying to the music and experience a desire to bow your head or lift your hands. The hymn "He Touched Me" highlights this healing, whole presence.

It can be in response to God's *movement*. Jonathan Edwards' wife became weak for three days as the Second Great Awakening began to sweep across the nation.

It may in the *presence of evil*. A feeling of agitation, guardedness, or need to be under the cloak of God's protection may flood your soul. I once walked into a new college religion class and experienced many of these emotions within the first five minutes. This was an enormously unusual moment, for I always begin my semester-long classes with confidence and optimism. Time bore out my spiritual suspicions, and this turned out to be a memorable class with an uncommon number of classroom management issues (not normally a problem at all for me) and the most cases of academic dishonesty I've ever experienced in a lifetime of academia.

You may experience a response to God's *direction*. Eric Liddell, the Olympic gold medalist, wrote, "God made me fast. And when I run, *I feel his pleasure*." His athletic skill and talent was used as a pulpit for the expression of his faith in Christ.

Finally, it can be a *knowing awareness of the Spirit of God in others*. When the pregnant Virgin Mary visited equally pregnant Elizabeth in Judah, the baby within Elizabeth (John the Baptizer) "leaped for joy." Elizabeth then blessed Mary as the mother of her Lord.[5]

A spirit-being can often recognize the state of the spirit in another. When Ted Beam was a young man, a number of persons prayed for him for years, particularly a woman named Anna Jean. On the Friday before he left college for Christmas break in his senior year, he accepted Christ. He hadn't yet told anyone when he arrived at his family's church on Sunday morning. As he entered the sanctuary, he was startled to be welcomed with a hug by Anna Jean, who began weeping and repeating over and over, "You took my Jesus. You took my Jesus."

How did she know? Her spirit witnessed with his spirit. Deep calls unto deep. It assured Ted that his experience with Christ was genuine.

The Body of Christ: Touching Others for God

Touch is ministry. It is action-oriented service. The telephone company used to have an advertising slogan appropriate to the mission of the church. The marketing mantra was "reach out and touch someone."

In Christianity, we believe all of us are ministers. Luther

referred to it as "the priesthood of all believers." One of the best definitions of *ministry* is to meet needs and help people grow into their God-given potential. Because individuals are so unique, your strategy for loving others has to have its own particular contours and design. Sometimes our love is just plain ambivalent. We talk love and act indifferent. In that regard, we are the fourth grade class that sent a get-well card to their teacher who was at home recovering from surgery. The card read, "Your class wishes you a speedy recovery–by a vote of 15-14!"

Cultivating this spiritual sense is meant for the use of others in the Christ's body. Like skin, the largest organ, the body of Christ is the greatest place of ministry. We're all in this together. As Herman Melville once wrote:

> We cannot live for ourselves alone. Our lives are connected by a 1000 invisible threads, and along these sympathetic fibers, our actions run as causes and returns to us as results.

When the roots of trees touch, there is an unknown fungus present that links together even trees of dissimilar species. The forest can be linked together, as one tree has water, another access to sunlight, and yet another to fertile soil. They share with each other and the whole forest benefits. This is how Christians can and should act in the body of Christ.

The kinesthetic side of touch may manifest itself in a number of ways in the church. It may represent *awareness*.

A journalist once asked Mother Theresa why she didn't give her time and attention to persons more worthy of rehabilitation in Calcutta. After all, her patients were likely to die within weeks. Mother Theresa's sense of awareness was keenly displayed in her answer. "These people have been treated all their lives like dogs. Their greatest disease is a sense that they are unwanted. Don't they have the right to die like angels?"[6]

Once you have been made aware by the touch of the Holy Spirit, you can't go back to ignorance. Many a Christian has returned from a mission trip to find a drive and a fire in their bellies to spend their lives helping the less fortunate. It's no accident that Mother Theresa and her staff would spend a great deal of time loving, bathing, and touching this lowest caste of people called the "untouchables."

Kinesthetic perception in ministry can involve *impression*. You have a "sense" that God is going to do something. When David Seamands pastored Wilmore United Methodist Church, host church to Asbury College and Asbury Theological Seminary, he generally preached in carefully (and prayerfully) prepared and planned sermon series. Once started, he rarely deviated from the printed order of sermon topics.

In early 1970, he was filled with a sense that God was moving via the Holy Spirit and that something was indeed about to happen. He interrupted the sermon series and preached a message entitled "God Is Just Around the Corner." Shortly thereafter came the famous Asbury Revival, where many thousands were drawn to the manifest presence of God in the Hughes Auditorium at Asbury College.

Symbolism may indeed be a part of this sense. Prophets such as Ezekiel, Jeremiah, Isaiah, Hosea, and others were directed by God to do quite odd activities, humanly speaking, to portray God's message to the people. These portrayals naturally captured all the senses. Visual and auditory senses were certainly employed, but the kinesthetic sense of movement was the greatest of all. They were like divine actors who through motions touched the heart of those willing to believe.

Finally, there is most surely an *action* component to this category of spiritual ministry. Frank Laubach would be compelled to pray "shooting prayers," directed towards leaders in worship, and he would see the entire spiritual atmosphere of a congregation become uplifted.

More than likely, it will involve incarnational effort, becoming Christ in that moment. Ann Gilbert explains the need in a moment with her daughter:

To help our four-year-old daughter overcome her fear of the

dark, her father and I always reassured her at bedtime that God was watching over her. One night after I had gone to bed, I felt a soft tap on my shoulder. "Mommy," a familiar small voice spoke up, "I know God's in there with me, but I need somebody with skin."

People need "somebody with skin." That person is meant to be you.

Some Additional Thoughts for Kinesthetics:

1) Be aware of those persons God is leading into your "radar screen." As you walk circumspectly (Ephesians 4:15), ask God who you are to reach out and touch today. This is a regular pattern of my life, and I stay amazed at the kinesthetic Spirit of God bringing people into my path for ministry.

2) Wes Seeliger says the church is often guilty of "loving humanity, but not people."[7] Have you ever been guilty of loving the human race, but not loving the individuals who are in your life?

3) Remember, prayer "touches" people wherever they are in the world. Even if you're not near them physically, you can still impact them spiritually.

God guides us first through his Word, then through our heartfelt desires, then the wise counsel of others, and then our circumstances. At that point we must rely on our own sound judgment…God gave each of us a brain, and he expects us to put it to good use.

-Bruce K. Waltke

God assumed from the beginning that the wise of the world would view Christians as fools…and he has not been disappointed…Have the courage to have your wisdom regarded as stupidity.

- Supreme Court Justice Antonin Scalia

A moment's insight is sometimes worth a life's experience.

- Oliver Wendell Holmes

Too many wish to be happy before becoming wise.

- Madame Necker

To know God's will is man's greatest treasure; to do his will is life's greatest pleasure. The Almighty does nothing without reason, though the frail mind of man cannot explain the reason.

- Augustine of Hippo

The young man knows the rules, but the old man knows the exceptions.

- Oliver Wendell Holmes

That the God of our Lord Jesus Christ, the Father of glory, may give to you the Spirit of wisdom and revelation in the knowledge of Him.

- Ephesians 1:17

Chapter Eight
Wisdom The Sixth Sense

There really is such a thing as a sixth sense. It may be a kind of uncanny intuition about what direction to take. It can be an abiding confidence regarding a decision. This sense can most surely be developed, because it has to do with accumulated wisdom. And wisdom comes from being with God.

Presence

Knowledge is horizontal; wisdom is vertical—it comes from above.

- Billy Graham

Paul's letter to the Ephesians differentiates between two words commonly defined together. Ephesians 1:3-12 is really one long sentence, and midway through it (verse 8) Paul writes that Christ abounds towards us in all wisdom and sound sense. Wisdom, or *sophia* in the Greek language, refers to a knowledge of spiritual matters. Sound sense or *phroneia* is a knowledge of practical concerns.

Christ wants to give us both the understanding and then the strategy to act upon what we know is true. We're not to be like the man who was so heavenly minded that he was no earthly good. In fact, because we are heavenly minded, we are able to do the most good.

This won't make sense to much of the world. That truth is relative to Jesus, a beaten and battered Jew from Nazareth, doesn't register to many individuals. It may seem odd, outdated, or outlandish. But Christianity is not so much a rational religion as it is a revealed religion.

The Apostle Paul wrote,

For the message of the cross is foolishness to those who are perishing, but to us who are being saved it is the power of God. For us it is written: "I will destroy the wisdom of the wise, and bring to nothing the understanding of the prudent."

Because the foolishness of God is wiser than men, and the weakness of God is stronger than men.

But God has chosen the foolish things of the world to put to shame the wise and God has chosen the weak things of the world to put to shame the things which are mighty.

But of Him you are in Christ Jesus, who became for us wisdom from God—and righteousness and sanctification and redemption.[1]

This sixth sense of wisdom and practical application comes from living in the *presence* of God.

It's not necessarily mysterious, but you do have to be alive to God. Bill Hybels once wrote,

> A few years ago a low budget movie became a box office smash. The story line followed a boy who had a mysterious capacity to see what other people could not see—in this case seeing and interacting with people who weren't alive. The famous line in this movie, The Sixth Sense, was the boy's revelation, "I see dead people." It's eerie but quite memorable. A pastor said to me, "Big deal. I see that at every deacons' meeting."

Leaders, too, have a special intuition- a sixth sense, if you will. We probably all know leaders whose internal compass consistently works better than anyone else's in the room. Everyone else is trying to find the right direction in a particular circumstance, and then this individual, who's been quietly listening, speaks up and suggests a certain course and everybody says, "That's it. Of course that's it. How did he or she do that?"[2]

Paul identifies the internal compass as "the spirit of wisdom and revelation."³ It is a right relationship with God for "the fear of the Lord, that is wisdom."⁴ Out of a lifetime of walking with God, we make sense of the world and how to navigate through life's potholes.

The longer I live, the more it strikes me that we live in a society of people lacking this sense. They really don't know where they are at. "All like sheep have gone astray. We have turned, every one, to his own way," wrote Isaiah.⁵ God spoke to Jonah of people who didn't know their right hand from their left.⁶

There is a chronic lack of wisdom. We turn in to the TV to talk shows to hear thrice-divorced actresses at thirty tell us how to manage our relationships. We hope to win the lottery though the chances of winning are astronomical. One man in my state said he was beginning to understand how the lottery would help education in Kentucky. He said, "Every time I buy a losing ticket, I get a little smarter."

I heard a speaker once tell how he was preparing to address a large convention. Before going on, he was pacing back and forth in a room, working off excess energy. A woman walked into the room, looked at him and asked rather directly, "What are you doing here?"

He replied, "I'm going to give a speech in a few minutes."

"Are you nervous?" she inquired.

"No, I never really get nervous," he said.

The woman raised an eyebrow and then said, "O, really? Then why are you pacing in the ladies rest room?"

He didn't know where he was.

National Geographic magazine conducted a poll of 1500 adults in each of nine countries to see if people could identify sites on an unmarked world map. US adults ranked sixth out of the nine nations in identifying sixteen places on the world map. Young adults eighteen to twenty-four ranked last in the world in this skill. Fourteen percent of young American adults couldn't find their own country on the map.

People don't know where they are. They may well lack wisdom and sound sense. Their internal compass is skewed. And it's not just a personal problem. It has world wide implications. E. Stanley Jones discusses its tentacles:

> At the center of almost every acute problem—personal, society, economic, political, and international—is moral and spiritual immaturity. The problems and the possibilities in almost every situation have outgrown the people. We are immature people dealing with mature problems. As often has been said, our intellectual lives have outgrown our moral and spiritual lives. John Foster Dulles tells how he was driven into being a Christian from seeing international conferences dealing with great issues break down because the people who took part in them lacked a spirit which would have made the conferences a success—a Christian spirit.[7]

When Borglum began his famous statue of Lincoln, which is in Newark, he took as his inspiration the practice of Lincoln during the dark third year of the Civil War of going out alone on the balcony at night to pray to God under the stars. The statue shows the brokenhearted president seated, his head uncovered and bowed in reverent meditation.

Wisdom starts with the presence of God.

Promise

Since developing wisdom takes time, it is essentially a promise. James put it this way: "If any of you lack wisdom, let him ask God, who gives it to all men liberally."[8]

Dallas Willard begins his awakening minutes in bed, giving the day to the Lord by praying the Lord's prayer meditatively and sometimes, the 23rd Psalm. It is his way of acknowledging that God is God and he isn't. That way he can give the day to the Lord and not be responsible for weather, traffic jams, irritable people, etc.

Craig Bryan Larson passed on a story by Timothy Munyon, who wrote,

> While living in Florida, I had several friends who worked cleaning rooms at a nationally known inn located directly on the white sands of the Gulf of Mexico. They spent their work breaks running barefoot in the sand. The problem was the inn required all employees to wear shoes at all times while working.
>
> I noticed the employees responded in one of two ways.
>
> The majority thought the rule restricted their freedom. The rooms had shag carpeting, delightful to bare toes, and just a few steps away lay the beach. To them the rule to wear shoes was nothing more than employer harassment.
>
> But a minority of the employees looked at the rule differently. Sometimes late night parties would produce small pieces of broken glass. Occasionally a stickpin would be found hidden in the deep shag piles. Some knew the pain of skinning bare toes on the steel bed frame while making a bed. This minority saw the rule as protection, not restriction.

Apparently wisdom as promise is understanding that God's ways are higher than ours. And, while we may not see some of the inherent dangers of going our own ways, they nonetheless lurk beneath the surface, ready to trip us up if we are wise in our own eyes.

J. I. Packer, in his book *Knowing God,* has as a central thesis that wisdom is first and foremost an honest recognition that much of what happens to us doesn't make sense. When we take off our rose-colored glasses, we see aimlessness, senseless deaths, and the evil prospering. In short, it looks like God is not in control. Once we stop asking the whys and wherefores that will never be answered this side of heaven, then, according to Packer, we are ready to learn wisdom. Real wisdom is following the promise by doing what we know we must do even when we are completely baffled by life's questions.

Promotion

Finally, we can look upon the acquisition of wisdom as *promotion*. The writer of Proverbs admonishes us to make it our life's goal: "Wisdom is the principal thing; Therefore get wisdom."9

Writer Alex Haley used to have a picture in his office that showed a turtle on top of a fence. Any time you see a turtle on top of a fence post you can be certain he had some help.

God sharpens our "sixth sense" over time and promotes us into places of leadership where we can be used for God's glory. Hybels believes, over time, a value system and world view becomes part of our paradigm base that informs subsequent decisions.10 Wisdom builds upon wisdom as "iron sharpens iron."

I have three offices that I use regularly. One is at my college, another is at home and yet another is at our get-away condo. Each office has its purpose. They all have books, desks, and chairs.

My office at Lindsey Wilson College is an incredibly ornate round office that's in the showcase Begley Chapel. I have my degrees and awards on the walls, and there I meet students and counsel.

Our condominium study is a place to get away and reflect and write. It's a wonderfully creative and quiet atmosphere.

My favorite office is my study at the home where we have lived the last fourteen years. It's upstairs, tucked away from everything. There are no degrees or awards there. It's my place to meet God on most mornings.

It's painted a peaceful color. As I sit at my desk, I can see to my left a painting of a Methodist circuit rider that reminds me of my calling. To my right is a peaceful ocean scene that reminds me how small I am in God's beautiful earth. In front of me is a plaque with 1 Corinthians 13 on it, reminding me that love is what it's all about.

I go there each morning around 5:30 a.m., unshaven and wearing sweats. I am a creature going to be with his Creator. It's where God comes near and bestows grace and wisdom. I realize there that it's all about God. Those who humble themselves will be exalted, and those who exalt themselves will be humbled. In Christian service, the wise know the branches that bear the most fruit are the ones that hang the lowest.

If God should decide to use you in his infinite wisdom, then know it's for God's glory. If you're given a gift, it's for God's glory. John Wesley, so honored and esteemed in his latter years, wrote in a letter to Francis Asbury, "O, beware. Do not seek to be something. Let me be nothing and Christ be all in all."

Augustine wrote: "Pride changed angels into devils. Humility makes men into angels."

The truly wise understand it's not about them. What goes up must come down. The rhythm of life is that sometimes we are in the key places of decision-making and sometimes we're not.

In the early 1970s, a movie called *Brother Son, Sister Moon* debuted. It displayed the life of Francis of Assisi. One scene was especially poignant.

Francis and three of his fellow monks walk to Rome in rags, worn and thin, hoping to get an audience with the Pope and obtain his blessing for a new order. This order, which they wished to begin, would be an order of poverty, devoted to service and love for others.

Finally, they arrive in Rome and come to the Vatican. The huge, ornate cathedral is filled with cardinals who have gathered in their splendid red robes and finery. It is a dazzling sight. At the far end of the cathedral sits the Pope himself on a mounted throne.

As the four ragged monks push through the crowd to gain an audience, they are held back by the Vatican guards. A commotion occurs as people yell to keep the beggars out. The Pope, from his vantage point, sees the press of the crowd and hears the noise and asks what is wrong. When told that some beggar monks want to see him, the Pope acquiesces.

Francis and his three ragged friends walked awed down the

center of the cathedral, flanked on every side by cardinals and other high ranking officials. As they gingerly walk up the steps to the Pope's throne, kneel and kiss his ring, Francis is asked by the Pope what it is they desire. Francis answers that all they wish to do is serve Christ with a new order that embraces poverty and service.

Now the commotion comes from the church officials. They become highly agitated about bestowing a blessing on these barefoot beggars and argue among themselves.

As the uproar surrounds him, you see the Pope look at the splendor of jewels and opulence and then back at these humble monks. Back and forth go his eyes and he's obviously in great internal consternation by the pained expression on his face. Then, to the astonishment of all, the Pope steps down from his grandiose throne, puts down his staff, and gets on his knees before Francis, the beggar monk…kisses his dirty bare feet and gives his blessing for a new order. This order would become known as the Franciscans and they would go on to impact the world.

Wisdom indeed is a sixth sense that can be crafted and grown to be something of great pleasure to God and to us. As the writer of Ecclesiastes put it, "For God gives wisdom and knowledge and joy to a man who is good in His sight.."[11]

It is a sense that comes to all who tend and nourish it with a right and renewed perspective.

The higher we rise, the more isolated we become; all elevations are cold.

- Marquis Stanislas Jean de Boufflers

I neglect God and his angels for the noise of a fly, for the rattling of a coach, for the whining of a door.

- John Donne

This eternal fountain is hidden deep. Well I know where it has spring, though it is night.

- St. John of the Cross

The religion [of some people] is something like the stars, very high, and very clear, but very cold. When they see tears of anxiety, or tears of joy, they cry out critically, "Enthusiasm, enthusiasm!" Well, let us go to the law and to the testimony: "I sat down under his shadow with great delight." Is this enthusiasm? O Lord, evermore give us this enthusiasm!

- Robert Murray McCheyne

Shame on those hearts of stone, that cannot melt in soft adoption of another's sorrow!

- Aaron Hill

Fire is the chosen symbol of heaven for moral passion. God is love; God is fire. The two are one. The Holy Spirit baptizes in fire. Spirit-filled souls are ablaze for God. They love with a love that glows. They believe with a faith that kindles. They serve with a devotion that consumes. They hate sin with a fierceness that burns. They rejoice with a joy that radiates. Love is perfected in the fire of God.

- Samuel Chadwick

Collapse in the Christian life is seldom a blowout. It is usually a slow leak.

- Paul Little

Chapter Nine
Spiritual Frostbite

In a book on spiritual sensitivity, it makes further "sense" to note there are periods when spiritual dullness occurs. The heavens may appear as brass. It might be called the dark night of the soul or spiritual winter. Having been an original native of the snowy upper Midwest, I prefer the term "spiritual frostbite."

I've lived in Kentucky, a border state just into the South, for the last half of my life. Here we close down schools if officials count more than six snowflakes. As I write this, we just finished up a cold snap, which meant the temperature dipped near freezing. The past week in Frankfort, our state capitol, it was so cold the politicians had their hands in their own pockets.

I'm used to the cold. I grew up in Wisconsin where there are four seasons—June, July, August, and winter. There's a short growing season, which is why I'm not too tall. I've been in 49 degrees below zero, so I understand frostbite. All humor aside, spiritual frostbite isn't very funny. When a coldness creeps into the soul, you have to know how to protect yourself and get warm again. Years ago I saw an article describing the progressive symptoms of frostbite. They are:

1. A feeling of extreme coldness;
2. The sensation of tingling;
3. Numbness;
4. The loss of all feeling.

If you ever hear the weather forecaster say there's extreme danger of frostbite, you need to protect yourself from the cold.

And if you notice any of the frostbite symptoms, you need to act quickly with counter-measures. The same is true for spiritual frostbite. The symptoms are essentially the same.

You begin to feel extreme coldness. You find yourself thinking everyone else is cold and unfriendly. Why are others apathetic? Why are they acting like the frozen chosen? Even God begins to feel distant. What we fail to realize is that whenever we point a finger at someone, there are three fingers pointing back at us.

It may not be that the group (and certainly not God) has changed at all. It's we ourselves who are slowly cooling, and we need to watch out—we're getting frostbitten.

Next, *the sensation of tingling takes place.* Spiritually, you still have some good memories of when your relationship with God was warm and friendly. And, oh yes, once in a while you get a warm, tingly feeling in church, but you notice you don't respond as quickly as you used to. Your spiritual metabolism is slowing down. Your soul sensitivity wanes.

Like the title of the Paul Simon song, you start "Slip Slidin' Away." You're not as involved in events that were once quite important to you. Your quiet time starts to be replaced by your interest in the newspaper or CNN. Somehow, spiritual activities have lost their place as a priority. You don't exactly know why… you just don't want to very badly. You're getting frostbitten.

Third, *eventually over time, spiritual numbness sets in.* Perhaps this is the real danger signal. At this juncture, you're surely frostbitten. Like Cain, when you go to church, you're in the land of Nod. You feel sleepy and distracted and your head starts to nod. It's like the mean old codger who got into an argument with the new Methodist minister in town. After much urging, the old man agreed to attend the church service the following Sunday. The young minister worked all week to prepare a sermon that would especially appeal to this man's logic so he'd believe in God.

The day after the church service, the two happened to meet at the local drugstore. The old guy said, "I'll have to admit it, preacher. I'll say this for your sermon…it kept me awake until the early hours of the next morning."

The minister beamed. "I'm happy that I succeeded in making you doubt the wisdom of your convictions," he replied.

"Oh, it wasn't that," the fellow answered. "You see, when I fall asleep in church, I can't sleep at night."

Usually when spiritual numbness has taken hold, you find your life, like the inn on the first Christmas, is too crowded for Christ Jesus in your life. He's just not a significant part of it.

It's because you become too busy. You're too preoccupied. There are too many other activities, none of them really bad in themselves. It's only that they crowd out the most important thing, which is soul care.

James Dobson describes this state as frantic overcommitment. The numbness is not only a psychological defense mechanism, but also a spiritual state. Gordon McDonald, when once speaking about well-meaning Christians, noted that if Satan can't keep you from good things, he'll instead get you too busy doing good things until you become fatigued and vulnerable. You become weary in well doing, and as a result, your heart loses its divine intoxication.

You find yourself saying this church or this community needs to be fixed or needs a renewal. Someone surely needs to do something. Someone else, that is, because you're stuck and saying it from a distance. You can't be heard. Spiritual numbness has now taken its toll.

It's a rather odd phrase to say that something has "taken its toll." A toll can refer to a charge or to a sound.

A pastor from Michigan said his church has a clean, ringing bell but it recently lost its toll. As community members were reminded of church by the tolling of the bell early on Sunday morning, the pastor noted its sound was very dull and so he sought out the bell-ringer.

Nearly an inch of snow and sleet had blown on it during a night storm, and consequently, it was thoroughly encased in ice. What a diluted witness it was. What a poor call to worship it gave. The pastor was impressed by the Holy Spirit that Christians can become sheathed in the sound-deadening things of the world, and as a result, their witness becomes ice-encased. Then spiritual numbness remains in winter all year long. As A. W. Tozer once wrote,

> Think about people who find themselves in religious ruts. They discover a number of things about themselves. They will find that they are getting older but not getting any holier. Time is their enemy, not their friend...They were not any better last year than they had been the year before.

Finally, you reach the final stage of spiritual frostbite, *the loss of all feeling*. Your sensitivity leaves you. You just stop going to church. You sleep in Sunday mornings. The loving feeling is gone and people in this spiritual state are the most difficult to win back to God. They are terrific at rationalizing that they're OK in the eyes of a holy God when in reality they're in a most precarious position.

That which would have warmed our hearts now misses the mark. Compassion and empathy that would be stirred within us by the Holy Spirit are replaced by a pale tolerance and tacit good will for others. Meeting personal needs and obtaining more become our life goals. And, when we give ourselves to our possessions, we become possessed. That which captivates our attention becomes an idol. And we become like it. We lose our feeling of spiritual sensitivity.

As the Psalmist put it so well,
> Their idols are silver and gold,
> The work of men's hands.
> They have mouths, but they do not speak;
> Eyes they have, but they do not see;
> They have ears, but they do not hear;
> Noses they have, but they do not smell;
> They have hands, but they do not handle;
> Feet they have, but they do not walk;
> Nor do they mutter through their throat.
> *Those who make them are like them;*
> So is everyone who trusts in them.(emphasis added)[1]

Brett Blair commented on how our preoccupation with a culture of gain undercuts our compassion and feeling for things that should matter. He wrote:

> Some years ago before the death of Mother Theresa, a television special depicted the grim human conditions that were a part of her daily life. It showed the horror of the slums of Calcutta and her love for these destitute people. The producer interviewed her as she made her rounds in that dreadful place. Throughout the program, commercials interrupted the flow of the discussion. Here is the sequence of the topics and commercials: lepers (bikinis for sale); mass starvation (designer jeans); agonizing poverty (fur coats); abandoned babies (ice cream sundaes) the dying (diamond watches).

The irony was so apparent. Two different worlds were on display—the world of the poor and the world of the affluent. It seems that our very culture here in the United States, and any other place that has a great deal of commercialization to it, is teaching us to live as the rich man in the story of Lazarus. We are occasionally presented with the images of the poor man Lazarus at our gate but we are immediately reminded of the next car we ought to buy and the next meal we should eat. We are slowly and methodically told it is OK to live our life of luxury while others live their life of poverty. But alas, it is not so! Heaven's reversal of fortune shall one day awaken us to the fact that we have separated ourselves from the agonies of others, that we did not care about others who suffered.

When medical staff in India wondered how lepers lost their extremities such as fingers and toes, they hired people to watch them for twenty-four hours. They discovered that, while lepers were sleeping, rats would gnaw on their fingers and toes. Because of their lack of feeling, the lepers weren't even aware it was happening.

Similarly, in a state of spiritual frostbite, our lives are nibbled away by various concerns and we don't even realize it. Of course, when there's no feeling, one is in danger of dying. When these symptoms have set in, we need to act quickly.

In case of physical frostbite, we are told to do three things:
1. Stay active;
2. Keep warm;
3. Stay in close proximity to others.

Once again, the cure for preventing spiritual frostbite is exactly the same.

Stay active. Be revived. Many times the Psalmist commands his soul to praise the Lord. The obedience comes before the feeling. Be proactive. You take charge of your soul and give your broken and cold self back to God. The writer of Proverbs put it this way: "Whoever has no rule over his own spirit is like a city broken down without walls."[2]

In a snowstorm, become active like an Eskimo who builds walls with the ice to provide a dwelling so that warmth can return. The action and faith come before the reviving.

Keep warm. Be ignited. John Wesley wrote that if a person will get on fire for God, people will come to watch him burn. If you get closer to God, you'll become warm for "our God is a consuming fire."[3]

John Ortberg once used a Martin Marty term called "a wintry spirituality" to describe how when the warmth and joy is gone from us, we need a way to get a hold on God when it feels as if God has let us go.[4] There is a way. Run to God and run away from distraction. Get to a quiet place where you know God is always there even if we don't immediately feel the divine presence.

Just as you'd rub your hands before a fire and move to keep warm, move before the fire of God. You don't have to just sit there. Mobilize and rouse your body and express yourself before the creative God of the universe. Eventually, you'll become reignited.

Finally, *we stay in close proximity with others and become redirected.* The question is often asked, "Can I be a Christian without joining a church?"

The answer is yes, it's possible. It's something like
- a soldier who doesn't join the army
- a student who doesn't go to school
- a football player without a team
- a tuba player without a band
- (insert your own analogy here)

You can be a Christian on your own, but here's the clincher. It's not likely you'll be one for long. There are no "Lone Ranger" Christians. The law of association applies here. You'll become like those you spend time with on a daily basis.

Proximity here means a level of intimacy, not just observing from a distance. The writer of Ecclesiastes asks a poignant question:

> Two are better than one, because they have a good reward for their labor. For if they fall, one will lift up his companion. But woe to him who is alone when he falls, For he has no one to help him up. Again, if two lie down together, they will keep warm; But how can one be warm alone?[5]

We need others. Stay in proximity.

Spiritual frostbite is a most serious matter. For the coldness of one or two or three can impact an equal number, and eventually the entire church cools off and loses the warmth of the flame of the Holy Spirit.

Decide to not let it happen. Be sensitive when the symptoms appear. A season of coolness, like winter, seems to appear in the lives of all saints. That is no sin. It seems to be the norm for Christian growth.

Frostbite is a deeper level, though and it can be avoided. Act quickly to be revived, reignited, and redirected.

HEART WORK IS HARD WORK. The crux of our heart-work towards holiness is our will surrendered to Christ so that God can take possession of it.

- Maxie Dunnam

Whether it be something tremendously important in our eyes or the greatest triviality, nothing, nothing may be so put between ourselves and Christ that it becomes a condition.

For in such a case we cannot surrender ourselves to him. The surrender must be unconditional; then—and this is a different thing from making prior conditions—we can pray for ourselves that our burdens may not be too heavy.

- Søren Kierkegaard

Do you want to enter what people call "the higher life"? Then go a step lower down.

- Andrew Murray

Bearing up against temptations and prevailing over them is the very thing wherein the whole life of religion consists. It is the trial which God puts upon us in this world, by which we are to make evidence of our love and obedience to him, and of our fitness to be made members of his kingdom.

- Samuel Clarke

"Life is like war," wrote F. W. Robertson of Brighton. "It is a series of mistakes, and he is not the best Christian or the best general who makes the fewest false steps. He is the best who wins the most splendid victories by the retrieval of mistakes."

Many desire the gifts of God but repudiate the demands of God.

- William Barclay

Chapter Ten
Spiritual Strength

E. Stanley Jones, author and missionary to India for many years, described once how Christians in his Indian district would gather weekly for a time of Christian fellowship called an *Ashram*. On that one day of the week, the few servants were let go for their day off and the Christians agreed to attend to the various necessary tasks around the church facility.

One of the tasks was the cleaning of the bathrooms. This was in the days before flush toilets. It was dirty job, and usually in Indian society, only the caste of the untouchables, the very lowest caste, would ever do the job. So, since there is no caste system among equals in Christ, E. Stanley Jones did his turn cleaning as did each Christian at the Ashram.

He noticed one week that Shandrey, a Christian convert from the Brahmin caste, the highest caste in the Indian system, never participated in the bathroom cleanings. One day he asked, "Brother Shandrey, when are you going to do the sweeper's work in the bathroom?"

The Brahmin replied, "Brother Stanley, I am converted, but I am not converted *that far.*"

If I could paraphrase Shandrey's comment years later, I believe he was saying, "I am serious about being a Christ-follower, but I lack the spiritual strength and resolve to do the hard things. I have hold of Christ yet, Christ does not yet fully have hold of all of me."

When Eugene Peterson wrote a book on his journey with God, he entitled it *A Long Obedience in the Same Direction: Discipleship in an Instant Society*. Peterson wrote,

> The people whom I lead in worship, among whom I counsel, visit, pray, preach, and teach, want short cuts. They want me to help them fill out the form that will help get them the credit.[1]

The Christian life obviously doesn't work this way. Just as it takes time to build one's physical strength, it takes much time, insight, and wise training to become spiritually strong.

In most African tribes, there is a period of initiation into manhood for boys. Some tribes take pre-adolescent boys (we'd call them "tweens") out of the village for a period of time where they are taught what it means to be a man by tribal elders. When the boys return as young men, they are baptized and told to go out in the village and act as if they did not know anyone's name. They are like brand new people starting over.

This is much like the person who converts to Christ. Jones thought it would be a lifelong process and that by age forty we'd all need to be re-converted. Why? Because by midlife we tend to settle down and lose our sense of expectancy and play for safety. Either our religion will be an acute fever or a dull habit, and for most it becomes the latter. An Anglican bishop surmised that the period of greatest spiritual casualties occur in midlife, not during the young-adult years of eighteen to forty. This is where the wind starts to go out of our sails.

This doesn't have to be so. As new creations in Christ, we can gain momentum and spiritual strength over time.

Soon after Augustine's conversion, he was walking down the street in Milan, Italy. There he met a prostitute whom he had known most intimately. She called, but he would not answer. He kept right on walking. "Augustine," she called again. "It is I!"

Without missing a beat and with the assurance of Christ in his heart, he replied, "Yes, but it is no longer I." Because of Christ and His Spirit, Augustine was a changed man. He was born again, a brand new creation.

There is a sense of what is called "spiritual synergy." It is a divine power that can be tapped into at any time. It is a kind of divine math where one (you) plus one (God) puts ten thousand to flight. Angelo Patri thus described it:

> Spiritual power is a hidden power, locked in the silence of the soul. We cannot force it to come at command of will. But when in extremity our strength is as water, our will as the sighing of the wind, when we yield all physical being and lean hard on the spiritual strength within us, the soul's strength rises to assure us as the sun rises over the rim of night.

This spiritual strength is man's inheritance, the eternal power granted him at the Creation. It is God's breath within him. On that strength we can go forward; we can take whatever comes and know it is well with us always.

The power is there for us. The Psalmist knew that God would bestow great strength on us.

> The LORD is my light and my salvation; Whom shall I fear? The LORD is the strength of my life; Of whom shall I be afraid?
>
> -Psalm 27:1

> God is our refuge and strength, A very present help in trouble.
>
> - Psalm 46:1

> Your God has commanded your strength.
>
> -Psalm 68:28

> Blessed is the man whose strength is in You.
>
> - Psalm 84:5

Psalm 119 gives a helpful pattern for gaining and maintaining spiritual strength.

> Verse 18: Open my eyes. Tune me in.
> Verse 25: Revive me. Turn me.
> Verse 28: Strengthen me. Train me.

Verse 32: I will run the counsel of your commandments for you shall enlarge my heart.

Tune In

Good insight not only prevents a person from being deceived by his own rationalizations, but forces him to face objectively the weakness and strength of his personal equipment.

- Gordon W. Allport

We must be wise in how we go about gaining spiritual strength. Thought comes before action. We have to do a strategic survey assessing three responses: ourselves, our adversary, and God.

We first note that our minds and bodies are actually at enmity with God. Paul's letters, particularly, describe how our own minds wrestle spiritually and often lose. He refers to persons with alien minds [2] and carnal (worldly) minds.[3] He speaks of individuals with futile thoughts and darkened hearts.[4]

To the Galatians, Paul revealed that struggle still goes on among professing Christians. To a degree, your old self (flesh) battles against your new nature (spirit).[5] Paul had his struggle himself, yet he ends with the victorious note that Christ will deliver him.[6]

Imagine when human beings were at their greatest strength and level of perfection. When Adam and Eve faced temptation for the very first time, many things were true of their situation that aren't exactly true for us.

They had no sinful heritage. No corrupted society. No television or internet. No dysfunctional family to blame. It's been pointed out there were many sins they couldn't even commit like adultery, stealing, dishonoring parents or bearing false witness against a neighbor. There was no evil, no trials, no suffering, no death. God's immediate fellowship was there for them.

They were created pure. But just as one rotten egg in a four-egg omelet ruins it all, one choice spoiled paradise. Something can be pure or impure, but it can't be mostly pure.

Adam and Eve, human beings at their best, were felled by

simple questioning. Essentially Satan whispered, "Did God really mean it? What did God say about eating from the tree of knowledge and seeing good and evil? Don't you want to be like God?"

They became so preoccupied with that plant in their garden paradise that they couldn't see the forest for the tree. And look what it cost them as a result.

If you think you are strong enough, spiritually capable enough fighting this battle on your own, you are seriously mistaken, dear reader. The Apostle Paul wrote,

> For we do not wrestle against flesh and blood, but against principalities, against powers, against the rulers of the darkness of this age, against spiritual hosts of wickedness in the heavenly places.[7]

Satan is much like an artist. He can paint sin in very attractive colors. He was half right. Adam and Eve's eyes were opened—to evil. And it affects all of us.

The great artist Rembrandt captured this truth in a painting, which displays Christ on a cross with an angry mob surrounding him. In the shadows is a man. The man is Rembrandt himself. By inserting his own face in the painting, he acknowledged his guilt and consent as well.

We are susceptible. We are all guilty. Satan will prey upon our weaknesses. Peter describes him like a roaring lion seeking to devour us.[8]

King David had everything going for him. He had looks, wealth, and fame. One night while walking on the edge of a place, he sees a woman (appropriately named Bathsheba) taking a bath. In a moment he is captivated. He tumbles for her and falls terribly into a trap of sin.

David didn't plan to all but ruin his life that night. He just underestimated his own heart's tug to sin and the evil force behind it. We're warned in 1 Corinthians 10:12 "Therefore let him who thinks he stands take heed lest he fall."

In other words, about the time you think you're strong, watch your flank. Beware. You'll probably be tempted.

Michael Boyland notes how we must know our adversary to be effective. He uses a military example from World War I:

> Aqaba in 1917 seemed impregnable. Any enemy vessel approaching the port would have to face the battery of huge naval guns above the town. Behind Aqaba in every direction lay barren, waterless, inhospitable desert. To the east lay the deadly "anvil of the sun." The Turks believed Aqaba to be safe from any attack. But they were wrong.
>
> Lawrence of Arabia led a force of irregular Arab cavalry across the "anvil of the sun." Together, they rallied support among the local people. On July 6, 1917, the Arab forces swept into Aqaba from the north, from the blind side. A climatic moment of the magnificent film Lawrence of Arabia is the long, panning shot of the Arabs on their camels and horses, with Lawrence at their head, galloping past the gigantic naval guns that are completely powerless to stop them. The guns were facing the wrong direction. Aqaba fell, and the Turkish hold on Palestine was broken, to be replaced by the British mandate and eventually by the State of Israel.
>
> The Turks failed to defend Aqaba because they made two mistakes. They did not know their enemy, and they did not have the right weapons.

Our weapons are simple. Turn from the enemy and turn to God through Christ through prayer who will do battle for us and within us.[9]

Gregory of Nyssa wrote,

> The effect of prayer is union with God and, if someone is with God, he is separated from the enemy. Through prayer we guard our chastity, control our temper and rid ourselves of vanity. It makes us forget injuries, overcomes envy, defeats justice and makes amends for sins.

Our first step is to tune in to a God who will strengthen us.

Turn Away

Be kind; for everyone you meet is fighting a great battle.

- Philo of Alexandria

Our next step in the Psalm 119 pattern for spiritual strength is to *turn away*. As you have turned to God, you must continually turn away from sin and its enticement. We are all affected by SAD. SAD is a seasonal affective disorder where people are impacted by lack of sunlight. SAD for Christians is lack of Son-light. It is a sin-affective disorder. It is a battle that surrounds us.

An unknown author comments on the highly regarded HBO miniseries *Band of Brothers,* which follows a company of US paratroopers through the preparation and experience of invading Europe on D-Day. Based on real-life interviews with survivors, the series captures both the intensity of war and the heroism of the troops. Lieutenant Richard Winters is a powerful example of a leader who understood his calling. While leading his troops into their most celebrated and challenging task of the war, combating the Germans in the Battle of the Bulge, Winters was approached by an exhausted soldier leaving the front line.

"Looks like you guys are going to be surrounded," the soldier said ominously.

Without hesitation Winters replied, "We're paratroopers, Lieutenant. We're supposed to be surrounded."

This is how the spiritual life is supposed to work. There are times of peace and times of great spiritual warfare. New levels, new devils.

Since you aren't strong enough on your own, you must understand the enemy's strategy to be able to turn and feign and appropriately retreat and assail when attacked. Satan follows particular strategies, and we can learn to turn through the stories of Scripture.

Doubt is commonly employed. Adam and Eve went through questioning that caused them to doubt both God's intentions and what God actually said.

Delay is another tactic. How hard it is to wait. Daniel speaks of encountering an angel who was delayed by evil (prince of the kingdom) from coming to Persia until the archangel Michael helped him.[10] Sometimes our very prayers, like that of Daniel, are impeded from being answered. When we are delayed, we tend to lose heart.

Distortion is what Satan is most capable of doing. While God is a creative, life-giving force, evil skews plans for good and wholeness.

Denigration refers to the little whispers and intrusive thoughts that consistently come your way and cause you to settle for far less than your potential.

Destruction is the ultimate goal. "A roaring lion" who seeks to devour and destroy.

If you expect these kinds of tactics will be employed, then you won't be caught off guard. After Jesus experienced his temptations in the wilderness, we are told "[the devil] departed from Him until *an opportune time* (emphasis added)."[11] Since even Jesus would be tempted again, we must not be "ignorant of [Satan's] devices."[12]

Our task is to turn away. When we turn, God provides a way of escape. Paul described this in his first Corinthian letter:

> No temptation has overtaken you except such as is common to man; but God is faithful, who will not allow you to be tempted beyond what you are able, but with the temptation will also make the way of escape, that you may be able to bear it.[13]

We each have moments of opportunities to decide whether to turn—or to give in to temptation. J. William Chapman wrote,

> Temptation is the tempter looking through the keyhole into the room where you are living; sin is your drawing back the bolt and making it possible for him to enter.

Just as prevenient grace gives us strength to turn from sin and turn to God, that grace is always there for us so we don't open the door to sin. God told Cain that "sin lay at the door."[14]

John Ortberg described a guy who works with cobras and other snakes at a zoo. He notes that when you capture a snake, there is a special technique of which you need to be aware. More people are bitten trying to let go of snakes than when they grab them. Like sin, Ortberg says. Easy to grab, hard to let go.[15]

Turn away. God will help you let go.

Train

We've been speaking of a kind of Christian "resistance training." Our task is to "submit to God. Resist the devil and he will flee."[16] In physical exercise, weight resistant training is where you use your own body weight or free weights to strengthen your muscles. It isn't enough to try to do this well. One must train in order to build strength.

The great spiritual fathers and mothers of the faith knew that *surrender* was the key to being strong in God. Paul wrote, "My strength is made perfect in weakness."[17]

He further describes, "Not that we are sufficient of ourselves to think of anything as being from ourselves, but our sufficiency is from God."[18]

Strength comes from surrender. Yielding to God and letting God work. Laying your weight on the weight of the universe as revealed by God.

In principle, this sounds simple. However, it takes a lifetime to surrender the depths of one's interior life.

E. Stanley Jones once told about a man who was showing a group how his dog could play dead. The dog was a great actor; his eyes were closed, jaw was open, and legs were stretched out. He looked completely dead, except that the very tip of his tail was wagging. And, this is true with us—the little allusions, the mannerisms, the bids for attention will reveal the unsurrendered depths.[19]

Let's learn from those who have gone before us. We aren't just to imitate Jesus, we surrender to Jesus. The early Christian creed was not "Jesus is our Exemplar," but "Jesus is Lord." Spiritual power is often not found, according to Jones, because we seek the power itself. Surrender is a kind of abandonment to the plans of God for your life.

You may well know of Larry Bird, the famous basketball player. Once, during a crucial game, his coach, K. C. Jones diagrammed a play on the sidelines, only to have Bird dismiss it. Bird said, "Get the ball to me and everyone get out of my way."

K. C. Jones shouted back, "I'm the coach and I'll call the plays." Then Coach Jones turned to the other players and said, "Get the ball to Larry and get out of his way."

That's the message. Give your life to Jesus and get out of the way. Surrender the ball and become part of a larger team effort that literally changes the world.

Philip Yancey once displayed how this truth is critical in any serious life-altering effort. He wrote:

The historian of Alcoholics Anonymous titled his work *Not-God* because, he said, that stands as the most important hurdle an addicted person must surmount, to acknowledge, deep in the soul, not being God. No mastery of manipulation and control, at which alcoholics excel, can overcome the root problem; rather, the alcoholic must recognize individual helplessness and fall back in the arms of a Higher Power. "First of all, we had to quit playing God," concluded the founder of AA, "and then allow God himself to play God in the addict's life, which involved daily, even moment by moment, surrender."[20]

Moment by moment. Could there be a better way to describe how we gain spiritual power? How can we become spiritually sensitive? In the end, we'll come to see that submission to God was central to sensitivity to God.

My prayer is that God will do this work of grace in you. May you run the course of God's commandments, so that God will enlarge your heart.[21] May your own spiritual senses be heightened. May you belong to Jesus Christ. And, when you surrender your body in death, you will then meet a familiar face and hear a comforting voice welcoming you into a fellowship where we will all enjoy the manifest presence of God for all of eternity.

Study Guide and Discussion Questions

Chapter One: Spiritual Sensitivity

1) How can you apply the revelation of St. Thomas Aquinas to your life?
2) When are you aware that your sensitivity to God is increased, i.e., your antenna is up?
3) What were some of your first God-thoughts as a child?
4) How does one exactly "humble him or herself?"
5) Have you ever felt God-intoxicated?

Chapter Two: Your Spiritual Senses

1) Before you took the quiz, what did you surmise was your primary learning style?
2) How does the way you're wired to learn and communicate affect your relationship with God?
3) Does your church's weekly worship service coincide with your major spiritual sense?
4) When have you noticed a "disconnect" with your spiritual sense and your church's effort to draw you closer to God?
5) Describe how the quiz validated or surprised your perception of your spiritual communication style.

Chapter Three: Eyes—Spiritual Awareness

1) How is the eye "the lamp of the body?"
2) How is it we're all afflicted with "Lowell's syndrome" before

coming to Christ? Can it occur after becoming a Christian?

3) Describe the spiritual blindness you experienced before crossing the line of faith.

4) Think of someone you know whose life is outside the family of God. How would knowing she or he is spiritually blind cause you to treat the person differently?

5) Comment on Ted Koppel's assertion that truth is often a "howling reproach" rather than a polite tap on the shoulder.

6) What can you do to develop a "God mind-set" so you begin to see God everywhere?

7) How does a Christian person guard his or her eyes in a visually-oriented poison culture?

Chapter Four: Ears—Spiritual Discernment

1) Describe a significant moment early in your Christian walk when you "heard from God."

2) How can you improve your spiritual discernment?

3) Does your life ever become stained by noise? Describe.

4) Christians, like newborns, usually have good hearing. How does spiritual hearing become dull over time?

5) What were some new insights you gained from this chapter about hearing from God?

6) Consider spending a day intently listening for the still, small voice of God.

Chapter Five: Smell—Spiritual Cleansing

1) Differentiate between initial cleansing and continual cleansing.

2) What can we learn from the Jewish practices of ritual cleanliness in the Old Testament?

3) When was a time you were really dirty and couldn't wait to clean up?

4) How does obedience relate to spiritual cleanliness?

5) How did you relate to the Spirit's work in a deeper cleansing of your "unconverted subconscious"?

Chapter Six: Taste—Spiritual Appetite

1) What are some evocative memories of smells you have associated with your faith journey?
2) How would your appetites reveal your interests?
3) Describe a person you know who has struggled with addiction.
4) Were you (or are you) especially tempted in early adulthood to stray from the path of Jesus?
5) How do we gain a true sense of self-respect?
6) How can we align our appetites in a way that will cause us to grow spiritually?

Chapter Seven: Touch Ministry

1) Can you talk without moving your hands? How are hands an important means of communication?
2) Why do we speak of "the hand of God touching us?"
3) How are our thoughts and feelings towards others conveyed via body language?
4) Describe a time when you experienced a spiritual "idiomotor response" to God's presence.
5) How do various liturgical movements in church and worship services represent "ministry unto the Lord"?
6) Are there activities or tasks you do where you've felt the pleasure of God?
7) Try Frank Laubach's "shooting prayer." Afterwards, ascertain if anything happened.

Chapter Eight: Sixth Sense—Wisdom

1) How does the "wisdom of this world" differ from spiritual wisdom?
2) Can you think of a time you did something that didn't make sense to someone who was only looking upon your decision with world-tainted reasoning?
3) Describe how wisdom and sound sense are interrelated.
4) J. I. Packer notes that a big part of wisdom is recognizing

that much of what happens to us may not make sense. Detail an experience you've had where it may never make sense to you in this life.

5) How can you sharpen this sixth sense?

6) What's the connection between humility and reason?

Chapter Nine: Spiritual Frostbite

1) Have you ever been frostbitten?

2) When was a time you had a season of "wintry spirituality?"

3) Why do we all seem to go through seasons of warmth and coolness in our relationship with God?

4) How would you describe a church that's "on fire" as opposed to a church that's "cold."?

5) How can a very few spiritually cold individuals impact a large group of believers? Conversely, how can a warm cohort impact a larger group?

6) What can be done to keep your spiritual temperature from consistently dropping too low?

Chapter Ten: Spiritual Strength

1) How far would you say you've been converted? How do you even measure this?

2) At this point in your Christian walk, where are you disappointed in your lack of spiritual strength?

3) Has your life been a "long obedience in the same direction?" Explain.

4) Where are you in the Psalm 119 patterns of tuning in, turning away, and training?

5) When are you more likely to cave in to temptation?

6) How are you thinking differently about training for spiritual strength after reading this chapter?

7) What else do you need to surrender to Jesus?

Endnotes

Chapter One
1. Psalm 19:1-4
2. sermons, March 2005
3. *Sermons of John Wesley*, vol. 1, p. 296. Sermon XIV. Mark of the New Birth
4. Ibid, p. 295
5. Ibid, p. 296
6. James 4:10
7. Matthew 18:4
8. Matthew 5:3
9. Matthew 5:5
10. Proverbs 3:34, James 4:6
11. Proverbs 29:23
12. 1 Thessalonians 5:18

Chapter Two
1. Terry Swan, *What in the World am I Doing Here?* (Belleville, Ontario, Canada: Essence Publishing, 2003), p. 14
2. John 3:3
3. Matthew 13:9
4. John 1:14
5. 2 Corinthians 7:1
6. Psalm 34:8
7. Proverbs 4:18

Chapter Three

1. Matthew 6:22-23
2. 2 Corinthians 4:3-4
3. 2 Corinthians 2:14
4. Luke 5:1-8
5. Matthew 5:8
6. John 14:19
7. Matthew 5:14b
8. Mark 8:22-25
9. Ephesians 5:15
10. John 1:51
11. Job 31:1

Chapter Four

1. 1 Samuel 2:1-18
2. Romans 10:17
3. John 8:47
4. John 10:2-5
5. Luke 8:4-15
6. 2 Timothy 4:3-4
7. Job 12:11
8. 2 Chronicles 34
9. Deuteronomy 30:14
10. Luke 6:46-49
11. Isaiah 30:21
12. Luke 9:27-36
13. Isaiah 55:8-9
14. Isaiah 59:1-2
15. Isaiah 50:4b-5
16. Jeremiah 33:3
17. 1 Kings 19:11-13
18. Psalm 23:1-2
19. Jeremiah 47:6
20. Psalm 4:4b

[21] Luke 8:18a
[22] 1 John 5:14

Chapter Five

[1] Adapted from Claudia Dreifus. "The Sweet Smell of Success," *The ARRP Bulletin* (October 2005), pp. 26-27.

[2] Matthew 15:1-20
[3] Proverbs 30:12
[4] Malachi 3:2b
[5] 1 John 1:9
[6] Isaiah 1:18b
[7] Isaiah 43:25
[8] John 15:3-4a
[9] Psalm 24:3-4
[10] James 4:8

[11] Craig Brian Larson, *Choice Contemporary Stories and Illustrations* (Grand Rapids MI: Baker Books, 1998), p. 40

[12] Ibid, p. 206
[13] Isaiah 1:16
[14] Hebrews 12:29
[15] Hebrews 9:15
[16] 2 Corinthians 7:1

[17] E. Stanley Jones, *A Song of Ascents* (Nashville, TN: Abingdon Books, 1968), p. 51

[18] Galations 5:16-17

[19] Skevington Wood, *The Burning Heart* (Minneapolis, MN: Bethany Fellowship Books, 1978), p. 265

[20] *Sermons of John Wesley,* vol. II, p. 389, Sermon XLVII. "The Repentance of Believers."

[21] Jones, *Song of Ascents*, p. 55
[22] Hebrews 12:1

Chapter Six

[1] Luke 24:30-35
[2] Revelation 22:1-2, 17
[3] Psalm 34:8

4 John 4:34

5 John 6:35

6 Revelation 2:7b

7 Revelation 2:17b

8 Romans 16:18a

9 Craig Brian Larson, *Illustrations For Preaching and Teaching*, (Grand Rapids, MI: Baker Books, 1993), p. 124

10 Luke 4:1-13

11 Philippians 4:19

12 Philippians 2:5-11

13 1 Corinthians 4:9b-10

14 1 Corinthians 4:12b-13a

Chapter Seven

1 *Merriam-Webster Dictionary* (New York, NY: Pocket Books, 1978) p. 392.

2 Daniel Lapin, *The Lord's Language* (Sisters, Oregon: Multnomah Publishers, 2001) p. 58

3 Paul Brand and Philip Yancey, *Fearfully and Wonderfully Made* (Grand Rapids, MI: Zondervan Publishers, 1981), p. 137

4 Ibid, p. 138

5 Luke 1:39-45

6 Brand and Yancey, *Fearfully and Wonderfully Made,* p. 144. See this entire chapter on Skin and Touch for a wonderful description of kinesthetic perception.

7 Wes Seeliger, *One Inch From the Fence* (Atlanta, GA: Forum House, Inc., 1973), p. 16-17.

Chapter Eight

1 1 Corinthians 1:18-19, 25, 27, 30

2 Bill Hybels, "Sharpening Your Sixth Sense," *Leadership* (Winter 2002), p. 80

3 Ephesians 1:17

4 Job 28:28

5 Isaiah 53:6

6 Jonah 4:11

7 E. Stanley Jones, *Growing Spirituality* (Nashville, TN: Abingdon Press, 1953) p. vi.

8 James 1:5a

9 Proverbs 4:7

10 Hybels, p. 80

11 Ecclesiastes 2:26

Chapter Nine

1 Psalm 115:4-8

2 Proverbs 25:28

3 Hebrews 12:29

4 John Ortberg, *God is Closer Than You Think* (Grand Rapids, MI: Zondervan, 2005), p. 152

5 Ecclesiastes 4:9-11

Chapter Ten

1 Eugene Peterson, *A Long Obedience in the Same Direction* (Downers Grove, IL: Intervarsity Press, 1980), pp. 12-13

2 Colossians 1:21

3 Colossians 2:18 and Romans 8:5-8

4 Romans 1:22

5 Galatians 5:16-18

6 Romans 7:18-25

7 Ephesians 6:12

8 1 Peter 5:8

9 Edward Rowell, editor, *1001 Quotes, Illustrations and Humorous Stories* (Grand Rapids: MI: Baker Books, 1999) p. 381

10 Daniel 10:13

11 Luke 4:13

12 2 Corinthians 2:11

13 1 Corinthians 10:13

14 Genesis 4:7

15 John Ortberg. *Everybody's Normal Till You Get To Know Them* (Grand Rapids, MI: Zondervan, 2003), p. 177

16 James 4:7

17 2 Corinthians 12:9

[18] 2 Corinthians 3:5

[19] E. Stanley Jones, *Poise and Power*, (Nashville, TN: Abingdon Press, 1953), p. 73

[20] Philip Yancey, "Not God." *Christianity Today*, July 10, 2000, p. 2, Psalm 119:32